The Origins of the Second World War 1933–1941

'It offers concise and up-to-date treatment of a major historical topic using the results of recent research . . . this is a well-developed text.' *History Teaching Review*

'Clear, succinct but wide-ranging coverage of an important historical subject . . . Very well written.' *Alan Sharp, University of Ulster*

The Origins of the Second World War analyses the reasons for the outbreak of the Second World War, one of the most controversial historical topics. Ruth Henig considers:

- the long-term factors that led to war
- the effect of British appeasement policies
- the significance of American isolation
- the ambitions of Italy, Japan and Russia.

This second edition has been updated and expanded throughout to take into consideration the most up-to-date historical research and now includes a Guide to Further Reading.

Ruth Henig was Senior Lecturer in History and Dean of Arts and Humanities at the University of Lancaster until her retirement in 2002. Her other books include *The Origins of the First World War* (3rd edition, 2002) and *The Weimar Republic* (1998).

LANCASTER PAMPHLETS

The Origins of the Second World War 1933–1941

Second edition

Ruth Henig

Routledge
Taylor & Francis Group

LONDON AND NEW YORK

First published 1985
by Methuen & Co. Ltd

Reprinted 1991, 1992, 1994, 2002, 2003
by Routledge
2 Park Square, Milton Park, Abingdon, Oxon OX14 4RN

Simultaneously published in the USA and Canada
by Routledge
270 Madison Ave, New York NY 10016

Second edition published 2005

Routledge is an imprint of the Taylor & Francis Group

© 1985, 2005 Ruth Henig

Typeset in 10½/12pt Bembo by Florence Production Ltd,
Stoodleigh, Devon
Printed and bound in Great Britain by
TJ International Ltd, Padstow, Cornwall

British Library Cataloguing in Publication Data
A catalogue record for this book is available from the British Library

Library of Congress Cataloging in Publication Data
Henig, Ruth B. (Ruth Beatrice)
The origins of the Second World War, 1933–41/Ruth Henig. – 2nd
ed.
p. cm. – (Lancaster pamphlets)
Includes bibliographical references and index.
1. World War, 1939–1945 – Causes. I. Title. II. Series.
D741.H43 2004
940.53′11–dc22
2004014254

ISBN 0–415–33261–3 (hbk)
ISBN 0–415–33262–1 (pbk)

Contents

Foreword

Lancaster Pamphlets offer concise and up-to-date accounts of major historical topics, primarily for the help of students preparing for Advanced Level examinations, though they should also be of value to those pursuing introductory courses in universities and other institutions of higher education. Without being all-embracing, their aims are to bring some of the central themes of problems confronting students and teachers into sharper focus than the textbook writer can hope to do; to provide the reader with some of the results of recent research which the textbook may not embody; and to stimulate thought about the whole interpretation of the topic under discussion.

Acknowledgements

This revised edition of *The Origins of the Second World War* owes much to my former colleagues in the History Department at Lancaster University and to all the students it was my pleasure to teach on my special subject on inter-war British foreign policy. I would also like to thank my husband Jack for his patient and unfailing support over the past seventeen years. The pamphlet is dedicated to the memory of two of my grandparents, two uncles and two aunts who died in concentration camps during the war. I never had the opportunity to know them, but they and all the other victims of the Holocaust will never be forgotten.

Timeline of key events

30 January 1933 Hitler becomes Chancellor of Germany

October 1933 Germany withdraws from League of Nations Disarmament Conference and announces intention to leave the League

January 1934 Germany and Poland conclude a ten-year non-aggression pact

July 1934 Attempted Nazi coup in Austria and murder of Austrian Chancellor Dollfuss

August 1934 Death of German President Hindenburg. Hitler replaces him as Führer of the German people, in addition to being Chancellor, and all serving German military personnel have to swear oath of personal loyalty to him

September 1934 Russia joins the League of Nations

October 1934 Murder of French Foreign Minister Barthou and King Alexander of Yugoslavia at Marseilles by Croatian terrorist

January 1935 In a League of Nations plebiscite, the Saar inhabitants vote overwhelmingly for incorporation into Germany

March 1935	Goebbels announces establishment of German military air force and a week later the Germans reveal plans for the reintroduction of universal military conscription to raise a 36-division army totalling half a million men
April 1935	Stresa conference takes place between Italy, France and Britain. The three countries condemn German rearmament, affirm their interest in the independence of Austria and in the continuation of the 1925 Locarno agreements
May 1935	France and Russia conclude a mutual assistance pact
June 1935	Britain and Germany sign a naval agreement, by which Germany's naval strength is to be limited to 35 per cent of Britain's surface fleet strength and 45 per cent of its submarine strength
October 1935	Italian troops invade Abyssinia. The invasion is condemned by the League of Nations, which imposes economic sanctions on Italy, but not including at this stage oil or an economic blockade
December 1935	British Foreign Secretary Hoare and French Prime Minister Laval agree to a partition of Abyssinia, but the terms of the 'pact' are leaked, and the plan is denounced in Britain, leading to Hoare's resignation
February 1936	French Chamber of Deputies and Senate ratify Franco-Soviet pact
6 March 1936	Belgium renounces its treaty of guarantee with France which had been in effect since 1920
7 March 1936	German remilitarization of the Rhineland, ostensibly in retaliation at French ratification of Soviet pact
June 1936	Popular Front government formed in France
July 1936	Outbreak of Spanish Civil War
August 1936	Goering given extensive powers to prepare German army and economy for war within four years
November 1936	Germany and Japan conclude anti-comintern pact

May 1937	Chamberlain succeeds Baldwin as Prime Minister in Britain
July 1937	Japanese troops invade Chinese mainland from Manchuria
October 1937	Italy adheres to anti-comintern pact
December 1937	Italy announces her intention of withdrawing from the League
February 1938	Chamberlain and Mussolini agree to recognition of Italian conquest of Abyssinia and to withdrawal of 10,000 Italian troops from Spain. This agreement leads to resignation of British Foreign Secretary Eden
March 1938	*Anschluss* between Germany and Austria
Aug.–	Runciman mission to Czechoslovakia to find
Sept. 1938	solution to Sudeten German claims
15 September 1938	Chamberlain flies to Germany to meet Hitler at Berchtesgaden
22 September 1938	Chamberlain returns to Germany to meet Hitler at Godesberg
29 September 1938	Britain, France, Italy and Germany take part in Munich conference which agrees that Germany should occupy the Sudeten areas of Czechoslovakia, with an international commission to decide on disputed areas
15 March 1939	Rump of Czechoslovakia invaded by German troops after Slovakia declares its independence
22 March 1939	Lithuanian port of Memel seized by Germany
31 March 1939	British government offers guarantee of British assistance in the event of unprovoked aggression to Poland and then to Romania
April 1939	Italy seizes Albania. Britain extends a similar guarantee to Greece
22 May 1939	Italy and Germany sign Pact of Steel
23 August 1939	Conclusion in Moscow of Russo-German non-aggression pact
25 August 1939	Britain and Poland sign Treaty of Alliance
1 September 1939	German troops invade Poland
3 September 1939	Britain and France declare war on Germany

April 1940	German troops invade Denmark and Norway
10 May 1940	The Netherlands and Belgium are invaded by Germany
10 June 1940	Italy enters the war alongside Germany
14 June 1940	German troops enter Paris. The northern two-thirds of France are occupied, and southern France, with its capital at Vichy, signs an armistice with Germany and Italy
September 1940	Japan signs a Tripartite Pact with Italy and Germany
April 1941	Japan and Soviet Russia conclude a non-aggression pact
June 1941	Over three million German troops invade Russia in Operation Barbarossa
July 1941	Japanese troops invade French Indo-China
7 December 1941	Japanese planes attack the American Pacific naval base and fleet at Pearl Harbor
11 December 1941	Hitler declares war on the United States, which now enters the war

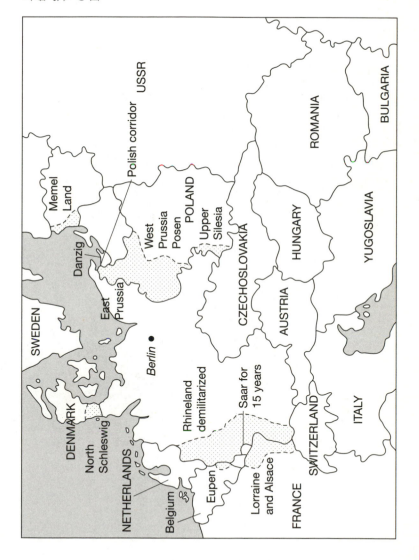

Map 1 Hitler's foreign policy: the struggle against Versailles – German territorial losses by the treaty.

Map 2 Central and
Western Pacific, 1921.

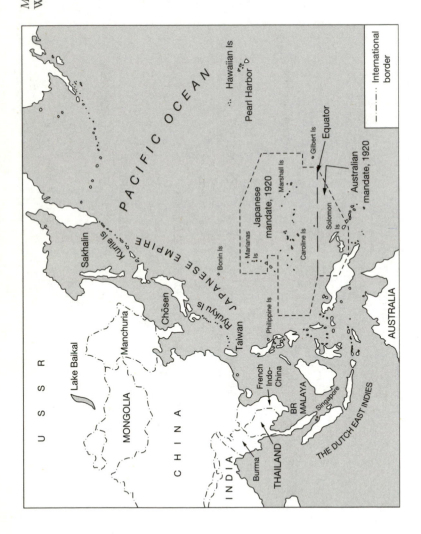

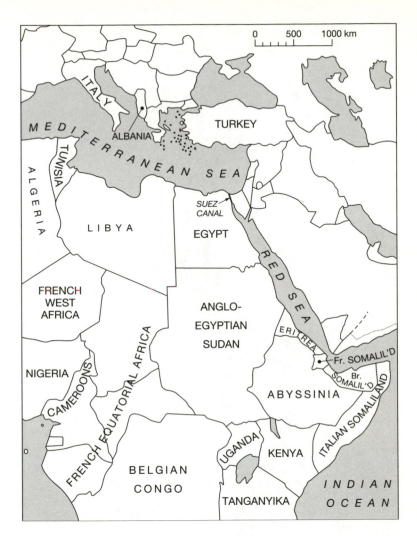

Map 3 The Italian invasion of Abyssinia, 1935.

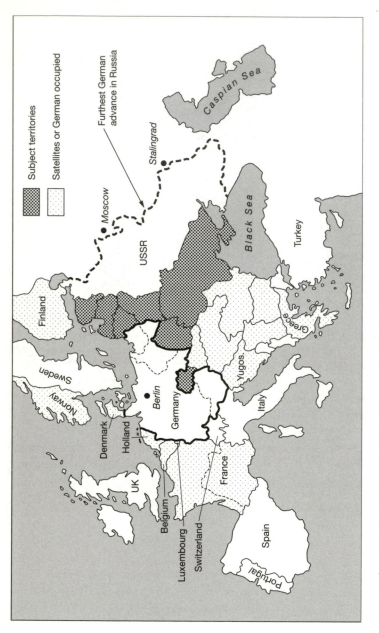

Map 4 The execution of Hitler's plans: Germany in Europe, 1942.

Introduction

In the past forty years, an enormous amount of material has appeared on the origins of the Second World War. Much of it has focused on the diplomatic events of the mid- and late 1930s in Europe, though more recently there has been an upsurge of interest both in the years immediately following the peace settlement of 1919 and on the wider origins of the conflict. It is no easy task for students to pick their way through this daunting mass of material, and to arrive at a clear view of the central issues involved in the outbreak of a European war in 1939, or of why this war escalated into a global conflict in 1941. Not only are there hundreds of volumes of official papers and documents issued by various governments covering the period, but it is also the subject of some fierce controversies and historical debates. To be in a position to form a balanced historical judgement on the origins of the war, and in particular on the role of Adolf Hitler, students need some knowledge of the different interpretations which have been advanced and of the nature of the controversies to which they have given rise.

The aim of this pamphlet is to present, as clearly as possible, the reasons for the outbreak of war in 1939 and for the worldwide escalation of the conflict by 1941, just twenty years after the signing of the peace treaties which concluded the 'war to end all wars', the First World War. Why did the settlements of 1919 prove so fragile, despite the strong sentiments of 'no more war' voiced so repeatedly by so many war-weary combatants and their families in the years immediately after the war? Obviously not all First World War veterans were supporters of the peace treaties, particularly those who had fought on what turned out to be the losing side, and not all set their faces against the use of force in the future to change some or all of the terms. We know that defeat came as a great shock to the German people and led to accusations of betrayal levelled at alleged 'traitors' who had sabotaged the German war effort and push to victory. Much of the published material in the past forty years has focused on the extent to which an Austrian-born corporal, who served in the German army during the First World War – Adolf Hitler – exploited such sentiments, organized a violently nationalist response to avenge the humiliation of defeat, and should therefore bear the prime responsibility for the outbreak of the Second World War. Clearly Hitler did not act in isolation, and much attention has been paid in recent years to the ways in which decisions were taken in Nazi Germany after 1933, the extent of collaboration with Hitler of the German army, big business and government officials, and the ambitions and motives of other national leaders, such as Mussolini, and the traditions and policy objectives of their governments.

The pamphlet is divided into four chapters. The first considers the long-term causes of the war, such as the political and territorial fragility of the post-war settlement, the economic weaknesses of the major European powers in the 1920s and the growing ideological divide which generated such strong social and political tensions both within countries and across the globe by the mid-1930s. The second chapter outlines the successive crises which led eventually to the outbreak of war in Europe in 1931, and to worldwide war by 1941. It considers Germany's European and world ambitions after 1919 and the impact of Hitler's rise to power. It examines the main elements of Hitler's ideological beliefs, and looks at the speed and scale of his rearmament programme after 1933, alongside the growth in territorial ambition of both Fascist Italy and ultra-nationalist Japan. The successive crises unleashed by the Japanese invasion of Manchuria in 1931 and the Italian invasion of Abyssinia in 1935 are considered alongside Hitler's remilitarization of the Rhineland in 1936 and the outbreak of the Spanish Civil War in the same year. This chapter then examines the impact of the *Anschluss* with Austria and crisis over the Sudetenland in Czechoslovakia in 1938, the invasion of Prague in March of 1939, and the conclusion of the Nazi–Soviet Pact of

August 1939, alongside Japan's invasion of China in 1937 and Italy's growing Mediterranean ambitions. The section concludes by considering the outbreak of war over Poland in September of 1939, and the way in which the escalating European conflict became linked with Japan's growing Pacific ambitions by 1941, drawing into the war in that year both the Soviet Union and the United States of America.

The third chapter of the pamphlet examines the many different interpretations of the causes of the Second World War which have been put forward by historians since 1945. Much of the material focuses on Adolf Hitler, about whom it is claimed that more has been written than about any individual in history other than Jesus Christ.

Was Hitler a degenerate psychopath, as King Victor Emmanuel of Italy described him in 1938, or 'probably mad' as Britain's Foreign Secretary in 1938 suggested, whose policies were bound to result in war sooner or later, or was his foreign policy acually 'that of his predecessors, of the professional diplomats at the foreign ministry and indeed of virtually all Germans' (A.J.P. Taylor)? Could British and French leaders have averted war up to 1939 by pursuing different policies, policies of deterrence, and by working more closely with Mussolini or with Stalin? Could they realistically have prevented German rearmament up to 1935 and the remilitarization of the Rhineland in 1936, and should they have stood firm over Czechoslovakia in the autumn of 1938, even if it meant war? And how important was the contribution of Italian expansionist ambitions and Japanese aggression to the outbreak of war in 1939 and to the subsequent worldwide escalation of that war? This chapter aims not to provide definitive answers to these questions but to provide a guide through the main controversies and arguments, focusing on the most salient points and helping students to form their own coherent and considered views on the main points of debate.

The fourth and concluding chapter consists of a bibliographical guide to those books and pamphlets which students may find most useful for their work. It is inevitably selective, but offers suggestions for further reading, either to give a more detailed general picture of the way events unfolded in the 1930s or to follow up on specific topics. It is extremely difficult even for specialists in inter-war international history to keep abreast of all the publications which continue to pour out on the period between 1919 and 1945; for students, the array of competing studies and textbooks now available must be very depressing! This pamphlet is my attempt to offer some guidance and a clear path through the maze.

1
Long-term causes

Many accounts of the origins of the Second World War focus almost exclusively on European diplomacy in the years between 1933 and 1939, starting with Adolf Hitler's appointment as German Chancellor on 30 January 1933 and ending with Britain's declaration of war on Germany on 3 September 1939 after the German invasion of Poland. Yet while the events of these six years are clearly crucial in any evaluation of the reasons for the outbreak of war in 1939, they cannot provide a complete explanation. The reason goes back to the Great War of 1914–18 and its impact, not just on the European nations who took part but on relations between Europe and the wider world. Winston Churchill, in the preface to the first volume of his Second World War memoirs, referred to the period 1914–1945 as 'another Thirty Years War'. This was because, as Philip Bell points out in *The Origins of the Second World War in Europe,* the disruptive impact of the First World War had shaken the political, economic and social systems of Europe to their foundations. And whilst the great powers of Europe, victors as well as the defeated nations, were gravely weakened by the long and gruelling conflict, the United States and Japan had emerged, from opposite sides of the globe, considerably strengthened economically and militarily. Both powers could, if they chose, mount a significant challenge to Britain's naval supremacy and to the worldwide territories of the British and French empires.

5

The significant shift in power from Europe to the United States, which was very evident in the 1920s, added to the complex problems faced by the major European powers in the aftermath of the First World War, and undermined attempts to achieve political and economic stability. Significantly, E.H. Carr entitled his study of the international relations of the inter-war period (written soon after the outbreak of the Second World War) *The Twenty Years' Crisis*. Whilst this sense of crisis was undoubtedly heightened by Hitler's appointment as German Chancellor in January 1933, it already existed strongly across Europe in the 1920s, and its elements were cleverly exploited by Hitler in order to gain popular support and political power. As we shall see, social tensions, economic weakness, ideological divisions and the political fragility of the new states of eastern and south-eastern Europe all contributed to the perception of a weakened and crisis-torn Europe. And at the heart of Europe, most crucially, the First World War had failed to resolve 'the German problem'.

A.J.P. Taylor, in his controversial account of the origins of the Second World War, claims that the war was 'implicit since the moment when the first World war ended', because of the failure of that war either to satisfy German ambitions or to crush them completely. His view is that 'The first World war explains the second and in fact caused it, in so far as one event causes another'. Taylor's book, published in 1961, was roundly denounced by large numbers of his fellow historians, principally because he focused his attention not on Hitler himself but on German expansionist ambitions and on the failure of successive British and French governments to check them. These ambitions, he argued, were there already before the First World War and remained strong throughout the inter-war period. Defeat in the First World War was regarded as a temporary setback and, according to Taylor, 'Germany fought specifically in the second World war to reverse the verdict of the first and to destroy the settlement which followed it'.

Few historians accept this analysis as it stands. Furious arguments have raged in the past forty years over the aims and objectives of different groups in German society: were the ambitions of army officers or officials in the German Foreign Office really the same as those of Nazi leaders? And was the principal thrust of German foreign policy in the 1930s simply to destroy the Versailles settlement, or was this destruction just a first step in a programme aiming at European or even world domination? These are issues which we shall consider more fully in Chapter 3 and, as we shall see, the question of the origins of the Second World War is far more complex than Taylor would have us believe.

None the less, Taylor is right to draw our attention to two important long-term causes of the Second World War – the fragility of the peace settlement which followed the ending of the First World War, and indeed the inconclusive outcome of that conflict itself. As he perceptively pointed out, 'The first World war left "the German problem" unsolved . . . she remained by far the greatest power on the continent of Europe; with the disappearance of Russia, more so than before. She was greatest in population . . . Her preponderance was greater still in the economic resources of coal and steel.' The peace treaty was concluded with 'a united Germany. Germany had only to secure a modification of the treaty, or to shake it off altogether, and she would emerge as strong, or almost as strong, as she had been in 1914'.

The First World War had left Europe economically weak and politically unstable. In the east, both the Habsburg and Romanov empires had fallen, and the vacuum had been temporarily filled by a succession of small, often ethnically diverse, new states – Czechoslovakia, Poland, Latvia, Lithuania, Austria, Hungary. Could these emerging small nations establish themselves with sufficient political and economic strength, at a sufficient speed to fight off renewed German or Russian expansionist ambitions? For the time being, German eastern ambitions, starkly exposed in the treaty of Brest-Litovsk, which was forced onto a defeated Russia in March 1918, had been thwarted – but by military defeat in the west of Europe, not in the east. Meanwhile the Bolshevik leader Lenin – helped by the German military command to return to Russia from Switzerland in 1917 – was in the process of establishing a new socialist republic in Russia, which served to intensify ideological divisions and sharpen social conflicts throughout Europe.

It was with the greatest difficulty that the victorious allied and associated powers managed to draw up a peace settlement at all. Within a year, the United States and Italy were disassociating themselves from it, and Britain and France were in violent disagreement over how it should be put into operation. For, as Taylor pointed out, the peace settlement was drawn up on the assumption that a democratic, republican Germany would cooperate in carrying it out. Many of its terms, relating to German disarmament and payment of reparations, could not be put into effect without German consent and collaboration. But the new Weimar government was too weak to secure that consent, and Britain and France were left with the problem of whether to impose the Treaty of Versailles by force or to agree to more lenient terms in return for German promises to carry them out.

Here was the first major post-war problem: Germany had lost the First World War, but large and important sections of post-war Germany accepted neither that defeat nor the peace settlement which followed it as a fair or final outcome. No German government in the 1920s could readily agree to allied treaty demands without incurring widespread public hostility. Enduring nationalist themes included 'the shame of Versailles', the 'war guilt lie', and the 'November criminals'. These Jews, socialists, communists and other traitors were alleged to have 'stabbed Germany in the back' by fomenting demonstrations and strikes in German industrial areas, thus preventing her army from winning the glorious victory which was so nearly within its grasp.

The Social Democratic Party, which shouldered the responsibility of signing the peace *dictat* and which tried to advocate some measure of compliance with its terms, lost electoral support as a result. The more right-wing political parties, which held the balance of power in Germany for most of the 1920s, never concealed their hostility towards the Versailles settlement and their intention to work for its gradual overthrow. Army officers plotted to evade the disarmament provisions in secret talks with the Bolshevik government, while industrialists in the Ruhr refused to hand over to France the required reparations quotas of coal and coke. It is true that, after 1924, Gustav Stresemann, the German Foreign Minister, carried out a policy of 'fulfilment' of the treaty terms, but only in order to secure a more rapid revision of those provisions affecting the settlement in the west: early evacuation of allied troops from the Rhineland and a downward adjustment of reparations payments. Once this had been achieved, Stresemann clearly had his sights set on territorial adjustments in the east. How extensive these would have been we do not know, but the Polish Corridor, Danzig and the Polish part of Upper Silesia were elements of the 1919 territorial settlement which no German government of the 1920s and no foreign minister accepted as more than provisional. It is significant that the new states of Poland, Czechoslovakia and Romania were referred to in Germany as *Saisonsstaaten* – states born to die within a single season: annuals rather than perennials like Germany or France.

Then there was the question of relations with Austria, many of whose inhabitants favoured the idea of some kind of union with Germany, even though a formal *Anschluss* or political union had been prohibited by the peace settlement. At what stage should Germany raise the possibility of closer economic collaboration with Austria as a prelude to a more political partnership? Furthermore, Austria, Poland and Czechoslovakia all contained large settlements of German-speaking inhabitants who had played a dominant role both politically and economically in the former Habsburg empire. Now they were minorities in states dominated by Poles or Czechs and Slovaks, or were inhabitants of a newly created nation called 'Austria', nearly half of whose population lived in the capital Vienna, many facing economic hardship and unemployment. What should Germany's attitude be to these German speakers living beyond Germany's present frontiers? Woodrow Wilson's Fourteen Points had promised self-determination for the people of the Habsburg empire, but not, it appeared, if they were German. Thus extreme nationalist groups within Germany were able to exploit Wilsonian idealism and draw attention to the grievances and future aspirations of Germans living in small countries surrounding Germany, and their campaigns could not be ignored by any German government seeking to maintain its electoral support. Sooner or later, territorial revisions would take place in eastern Europe either by agreement or by force; Germany would once more regain its pre-1914 frontiers, and possibly even unite with the Germans of Austria and Czechoslovakia. These were not just the idle dreams of extreme right-wing groups in Germany, but items on the political agenda for serious discussion by successive Weimar governments.

Not surprisingly, such ambitions alarmed French leaders. Had 1.5 million Frenchmen given their lives on the western front only to bring into being a more expansionist and dominant Germany than had existed before 1914? Inter-war French policy was therefore clear – to contain Germany as tightly as possible within the framework of the Versailles settlement, and to secure the assistance of its fellow victors in the enforcement of the treaty terms. But none of its wartime partners was willing to assist France. The situation

9

facing French leaders after 1919 was that, in addition to a deep-seated 'German problem' there were also difficulties in relation to American attitudes towards Europe, an enduring 'Italian problem', and worrying expansionist ambitions in China on the part of Japan.

The United States was emerging as the world's most powerful economy at the end of the First World War, and its President, Woodrow Wilson, had taken the lead at the Paris Peace Conference in framing the peace settlement. But he had crucially failed to secure broad support for his diplomacy back home, and as early as November 1919, and again in March 1920, political opponents of the President persuaded the United States Senate to reject the Versailles settlement, and any possibility that America would play any part in helping to execute the peace treaties. A new Republican President, Warren Harding, elected in November 1920, made it abundantly clear that his country expected prompt repayment of the sizeable war debts which the allied countries owed to America as a result of the long four-year conflict, but wanted no political involvement in European power struggles. Thus the one country which had the economic resources to help put Europe back on its feet in the 1920s deliberately distanced itself from all the post-war economic and political crises which beset the continent after 1919, and thereby seriously undermined allied efforts to restore stability.

A second wartime partner, Italy, was deeply dissatisfied with the peace settlement in the Adriatic and Near East. The Italian nation had been sharply divided over the merits of intervention in the war, and its military performance had been less than impressive. Significant gains at the end of the war were needed to justify mounting economic and social pressures, and though Italy did gain the Austrian Tyrol and Trentino region, and some former Turkish possessions in the eastern Mediterranean, the Adriatic port of Fiume was not included. Mounting resentment over what was increasingly referred to by nationalists as the 'mutilated victory', and a series of post-war social and industrial convulsions, destabilized the weak post-war Italian government, and resulted in the rise to power of Mussolini and his Fascist party. (For a fuller account see the pamphlet in this series by Martin Blinkhorn: *Mussolini and Fascist Italy*.) Their uncompromising message was that Italy had not received from its allies the gains to which its gallant war efforts had entitled it. Previous Italian leaders had kowtowed to Britain, France and America, and the result was that Italy had been treated with contempt and tossed only a few pitiable territorial crumbs. The Fascists would change all this and turn Italy into a power to be respected and feared. Mussolini's attempted forcible seizure of Corfu in 1923 showed how new status was to be achieved. Clearly, after 1922, Italy could not be counted on to assist France in the containment of Germany unless Mussolini received in return support for his own objectives of Mediterranean and North African expansion.

Meanwhile, Britain's Asian ally, Japan, was also pursuing an expansionist agenda. Its leaders had utilized the war, and the preoccupation of the European powers with the fighting in Europe, to make sweeping economic and territorial demands on the new republican Chinese government. In addition, Japan had occupied German concessions on the Chinese mainland, and German Pacific colonies north of the Equator. Japan already possessed extensive treaty rights and railway concessions in the northern Chinese province of Manchuria, and was also building up a sizeable navy. Whilst Japan became, along with Britain, France and Italy, one of the permanent Council members of the post-war League of Nations, its interests were sharply focused on the Pacific region, and on maintaining and extending its territorial and economic ambitions. Growing Japanese power threatened not just British and French interests in the Far East but American and Russian influence as well. Thus Pacific rivalries were an ever-present accompaniment to European problems throughout the inter-war period, and at crucial times distracted the attention of French and British leaders away from European diplomacy.

A further problem was France's former European ally, Russia. Lenin's Bolshevik revolution of November 1917 had sparked off allied intervention, in a vain attempt to keep an eastern front alive in the war, and then a protracted Russian civil war. After 1921, Russia was economically exhausted and at the same time politically suspect, the ideological leper of Europe. Even if its support had been wanted in the 1920s, Soviet Russia after 1919 had no common frontier with Germany, and so could only indirectly assist in policies of containment. Besides, it shared with Germany a long-term interest in the fate of the new east European states, large portions of which had been carved out of former Russian territories, and it was therefore conceivable that Russia and Germany might work together to undermine the whole peace settlement. The 1922 Treaty of Rapallo and a further treaty in 1926 concluded between the two countries

11

seemed to suggest that this was actually happening, much to the consternation of France. Successive French governments struggled to weld the east European 'successor states' of Poland, Czechoslovakia, Romania and Yugoslavia into a coherent political 'bloc' which could replace their former ally, Russia, and wield economic and military power to uphold the territorial settlement and contain Germany. But the political and territorial differences of the 'successor states' were as strong as their desire to check German, Russian or Hungarian resurgence, and all of them faced severe domestic problems.

This then left only Britain and, to successive French governments, Britain appeared to be a most selfish ally. Its main concerns appeared to be the survival and consolidation of the British empire, and the recovery of pre-war British trade. The first task consumed most of what military and naval forces Britain had, leaving little to spare for the enforcement of the 1919 settlement. The second depended on a peaceful and prosperous Europe, which in turn necessitated a rapidly recovering and contented Germany, who had been one of Britain's most important pre-war customers. But to promote recovery and gain contentment, German governments demanded far-reaching treaty revisions which would inevitably lead to a substantial recovery of German power. Many people in Britain agreed with the German view that aspects of the peace treaties were both harsh and vindictive and should be revised. (For further discussion of this aspect see the pamphlet in this series by Ruth Henig: *Versailles and After.*)

Thus, in the 1920s France worked for the containment of Germany and for strict treaty enforcement, while Britain sought German conciliation and treaty revision, leaving Britain and France in constant dispute and Germany ready to profit from the disarray. And yet the aim of both powers was the same; their overriding concern was to prevent the outbreak of another war like the one which had engulfed them in 1914.

They differed on the most effective means to secure lasting peace, but their prime objective was to avoid war, and their military spending was geared to defence and to deterrence. Both powers were, in a broad sense, satisfied with the outcome of the war as it affected their own territorial possessions. Both governments needed a long spell of peace to recover from the effects of the war and to regain their political and economic strength. The war had taken a heavy toll in deaths and serious injuries, and its vast human and material cost caused tremendous economic and social problems which post-war governments found difficult to handle.

The allied and associated powers had spent two and a half times as much to win the war as their opponents had spent to lose it, and in the case of Britain and France only a part of this cost was financed by taxation and accumulated assets. The majority of the finance was raised in loans from home investors and from the United States, and the servicing of these huge debts in the early 1920s consumed a third and more of the budgets of each of the two governments. On top of this, because of the widespread economic effects of the war throughout Europe, there were violent short-term currency fluctuations which hampered the restoration of international trade, and long-term depreciation against the American dollar. The return to the pre-war gold standard, insisted upon by the United States before credit would be made available to European governments, forced upon Europe deflationary economic policies which had serious social effects.

Labour unrest and industrial strife had been experienced in Britain and France before 1914. The early years of the twentieth century had seen the growth and consolidation of trade unions and the formation of political parties representing the interests of organized labour. Involvement in the war and the need to produce munitions on a vast scale increased the influence of workers' organizations, but at the same time the Russian revolutions of 1917 revealed the dangerous threat such organizations could pose to the established political, social and economic order. Traditional elites in Britain, France and throughout Europe felt their power and position threatened by the revolutionary forces unleashed by the war. The immediate post-war years witnessed a number of sharp social and economic clashes between employers and their workers, and between landlords and their tenants.

Such struggles were not confined within national boundaries but also assumed significant international dimensions. The convening by the Bolsheviks of the Second Congress of the Third International in Moscow in the summer of 1920 led to the formation on a world-wide scale of an organized bloc of communist parties, whose members looked to the Bolsheviks for inspiration and guidance. There were left-wing parties which refused to be bound so strictly by Bolshevik interpretations and instructions, and thus the forces of organized labour were fatally divided just when employers and landlords were summoning all the support they could muster, including gangs of demobilized soldiers, to overcome the sharpened post-war labour challenge. Thus not only did European countries find themselves internally weakened at a time when the payment of huge war debts and reparations was bound to cause significant problems, but there was also the emergence of an international ideological divide, cutting across national preoccupations, which became more and more significant as the 1930s approached.

In Britain and France, therefore, successive governments were preoccupied by domestic problems and tried to pursue policies which would conciliate the forces of labour and counteract the ideological attraction of Moscow. In Italy, social and economic divisions and the failure of existing political parties to find effective ways of dealing with them opened the way to the establishment of a Fascist government. Many of the east and south-east European states succumbed to right-wing dictatorships of one sort or another, or were polarized, as in Austria, between the forces of tradition, land and church leadership on the one hand, and organized labour on the other. There were in the 1920s attempted right-wing coups in Germany too, and, while these did not for the moment succeed, the massive currency devaluation which hit Germany in 1923 undermined social stability and caused widespread social and economic resentment.

German finances were stabilized only after American intervention and the floating of a massive American loan in 1924. This enabled Germany to pay reparations to France, Britain and Belgium, albeit on a much more modest scale than the French had originally pressed for, and enabled the former allies to repay their war debts to the United States. On more than one occasion the British government suggested the all-round cancellation of war debts and reparations, but neither the French nor the American governments favoured such a solution. Nor were the Americans willing to extend large government credits to Europe to help with the process of reconstruction and economic recovery. What they did do was to reduce interest on war debts, extend repayment periods and encourage private investors and corporations to invest capital in individual European firms and countries. Such investment in Germany between 1924 and 1929 enabled factories to be re-equipped and modernized, and industrial enterprises to be extended on a substantial scale.

The Wall Street crash of 1929, therefore, had a catastrophic effect on America's European debtors. As the depression in America deepened and loans were called in, the flow of funds to Europe stopped and capital was withdrawn. European investors then compounded the crisis by switching their own money to safer havens overseas or by cashing in their assets. Germany, a major recipient of loans, was bound to be severely hit, along with countries such as Austria and Hungary whose economies had been shaky throughout the 1920s. Unemployment in Germany in March 1929 was already standing at 2.8 million registered workers without jobs. By February 1931 there were nearly five million people unemployed, and a year later the figure had risen to over six million (around 10 per cent of the population but over 30 per cent of the work force). The German government, under increasing political pressure, pursued orthodox policies of deflation which resulted in wage cuts and further job losses. Though it was agreed that reparations payments could be temporarily suspended in summer 1931, a German proposal to conclude a customs union with Austria caused an international outcry which played into the hands of extreme nationalists in Germany, who were gaining increasing popular support. When Hindenburg, the ageing German president, came up for re-election in 1932, the National Socialist Party leader Adolf Hitler forced him to a second round of voting because Hindenburg had narrowly failed to gain an overall majority on the first ballot. ('Nazi' is an abbreviation of 'National Socialist' in German.) Hitler himself gained the support of over 13 million voters who were willing to believe his strident claims that the miseries being suffered so acutely by the German people resulted from the iniquities of the Treaty of Versailles and the international conspiracies of Jewish communists. Such a massive electoral following impressed army leaders and right-wing nationalist politicians seeking to form a strong government. It was repeated in the Reichstag elections four months later when the National Socialists secured 13.7 million votes and 230 seats (just over a third of votes cast). In the various elections held in Germany in 1932, the Nazis consistently won a third or more of the votes polled, showing that they had become a serious threat to the more established parties who were also facing an upsurge in communist support. Leading members of the German government, including army leader Kurt von Schleicher and the well-connected Catholic aristocrat Franz von Papen, decided that the Nazi challenge should be harnessed by bringing into office one or two Nazi leaders. After some hard bargaining in late 1932 and January 1933, Hitler was invited to become

15

Chancellor in a coalition cabinet which included two other Nazi Party members, alongside representatives of the more established and traditional right-wing and centre-right parties. Hindenburg was reluctant to agree to the inclusion in the cabinet of the upstart 'Bohemian corporal', as he disparagingly called him, to emphasize his Austrian and humble origins, and had to be cajoled into giving his assent. 'We will have him framed in' was the super-confident declaration of one traditional party boss about Hitler's appointment. It was to be one of the most resounding political misjudgements of all time.

We cannot argue with certainty that Hitler owed his political elevation entirely to the effects of the depression in Germany, though the evidence does appear to support this interpretation. Clearly the Nazis, under Hitler's leadership, were sufficiently organized to have exploited any internal crisis, though whether this would have resulted in such widespread electoral support, or perhaps have involved a more forceful seizure of power, we cannot know. Would the Weimar system of coalition governments have survived without the depression? Was it putting down roots in the later 1920s, or were internal divisions becoming more and more irreconcilable? (For further discussion of this topic see the pamphlet in this series by Ruth Henig *The Weimar Republic, 1919–1933*.) It would be wrong to see the years 1924–9 as a 'golden period' of peace and hope in the inter-war history of Germany and of Europe. Problems remained to be solved and serious tensions persisted. On the other hand, these were being contained by the various government coalitions, and challenges from right and from left did not pose serious threats. It took three years of severe economic dislocation and widespread social distress to bring about substantial political changes throughout Europe, including a national coalition government in Britain and a National Socialist Chancellor in Germany. Ironically, the economic situation in Germany was beginning to improve just as Hitler came to power. He was therefore able to claim the full credit for economic recovery.

2
The years 1933–41

Nazi ideology

Hitler's seemingly inexorable rise to power caused anxiety both within Germany and in neighbouring countries. For Hitler was no ordinary party leader and the Nazis did not behave like members of more traditional political parties. They laid great stress on visual and verbal impact – on uniforms, on emblems such as swastikas, on endlessly repeated slogans and on carefully staged parades and marches. The use of violence was an integral part of their struggle for recognition and power, and attracted as many followers as it repelled. Their meeting places were not only back rooms in cafés and beer cellars but also street corners and public open spaces where Hitler could harangue his listeners and whip them up into a frenzy, while his armed bodyguards beat up dissenters and political opponents. The party message was kept simple: traitors inside Germany had conspired with enemies abroad to defeat Germany in 1918 and to keep it weak since that time. The Nazis demanded that these traitors be replaced by loyal German patriots like themselves, so that Germany could be 'redeemed' and regenerated. In the short term, Germany needed to recover its strength and break loose from the shackles of Versailles. It would then regain its natural mastery of central and south-eastern Europe, denied to it in the 1920s by an international conspiracy organized by Jews and communists. With Hitler at the helm and the Nazis by his side, a greater Germany, embracing all Germans including those at present living outside Germany's present frontiers, would achieve its destiny through the establishment of a thousand-year Third Reich. (The First Reich had been the medieval Holy Roman Empire of the German nation, and the Second had been the German empire as established by Bismarck in 1871.)

Those who managed to read through all the turgid prose of *Mein Kampf* (*My Struggle*), written by Hitler while imprisoned in Landsberg fortress after his premature bid for power in the Beer Hall putsch in Munich in November 1923, could find these ideas developed obsessively and at great length. They were also scattered through Nazi Party publications and speeches given by Hitler and his closest associates in the late 1920s and early 1930s. A second book, even more explicit and obsessive than *Mein Kampf* in relation to Germany's destiny and to the factors which dictated the rise and fall of great powers, was written in 1928 though not published during Hitler's lifetime. But what all these writings and speeches had in common was an exaggerated emphasis on what Hitler regarded as the key determinants in human history: racial struggle and the survival of the fittest. As Ian Kershaw has pointed out, these two themes had been central to Hitler's thinking since the 1920s. And his obsession with race was combined with concerns about space, since his study of history had convinced him that successful nations needed to secure adequate living space and food resources in order to consolidate their strength and to expand.

Nazi ideology was fundamentally racist, based on the idea that a hierarchy of races existed throughout the world. The Aryan race, encompassing German and Nordic peoples, was the supreme culture-creating race while Slavs and Latins were lesser-value races. Other races, notably eastern ones, could carry culture but not create it, and yet others, such as the black races, were destructive of superior races and were incapable of being either creative or of carrying culture. Thus the Aryan peoples had a responsibility to maintain and to strengthen their racial purity – Hitler described it as their 'mission, ordained by God'. As he put it in *Mein Kampf*, 'We are members of the highest species of humanity on this earth, . . . we have a correspondingly high duty and . . . we shall fulfil this duty only if we inspire the German people with the racial idea, so that they will occupy themselves not merely with the breeding of good dogs and horses and cats, but also care for the purity of their own blood'.

Only a racially pure nation would possess the strength to expand and to win the struggle for survival against other nations. As another Nazi leader, Josef Goebbels, put it in the late 1920s, 'we must have a healthy people in order to prevail in the world'. A racially pure, invigorated and united Germany could then expand its territorial base into areas peopled by lesser races and ensure their continued domination by conquest of the resources, mineral and human, of these areas. As Hitler explained in his second book, domestic policy was the 'art of securing for a nation the strength, in the shape of racial quality and numbers, necessary to secure living space'. Thus race and space were inextricably linked; a racially pure Germany would inevitably expand and require more living space, or *Lebensraum*, in central or eastern Europe.

But such living space would not be won without conflict. A second fundamental Nazi belief was in life as a constant, ceaseless struggle for supremacy, for resources and for power. Their thinking was based on crude social Darwinist ideas about the 'survival of the fittest', in which the conclusions of Charles Darwin's scholarly researches into selection and evolution amongst plants and animals had been transposed to the social realm. According to this view, humans inevitably competed against each other, and the strongest and most biologically fit survived and dominated. Such competition was a basic element of the human condition, and was a never-ending process for individuals and for nations. As Hitler wrote in 1928, 'Wherever our success may end, that will always be only the starting point of a new fight'. Men and women had to be ready for the struggle, ready to fulfil their historic destiny and, in the case of the Aryans, ready to lead. War was an inevitable part of this constant battle to secure a dominant position and to impose power on lesser peoples. Failure to compete, failure to maintain purity, any under-mining of the will to win or degeneration of racial purity would lead to domination by others, and all the shame and dishonour that this would bring. This, according to Hitler, was the fate which had befallen Germany in 1918 when the German army had not been defeated in the field but had been prevented from winning the victory within its grasp because of betrayal by enemies within: communists, socialists and Jews.

The most dangerous of Germany's enemies, as far as Hitler was concerned, were the Jews. Hitler was virulently anti-Semitic, and had been since his days in Vienna before the First World War. But, by

19

fusing traditional anti-Semitic sentiments with his racial theories, Hitler portrayed the Jews not only as enemies of Christianity or as ruthless capitalist exploiters of the poor but also as racial defilers. He claimed to have discovered a pernicious Jewish virus, which, if not isolated, would contaminate German blood and cause 'national race tuberculosis'. He seriously claimed, near the end of his life, that his work in isolating and eliminating this Jewish virus was as significant for humanity as Louis Pasteur's success in isolating germs had been in the nineteenth century, and therefore that he too deserved to receive the Nobel prize. In Hitler's view, Jews were not a race as such, they were parasites who tried to fasten upon racially pure bodies and pollute their blood. Thus they had to be isolated and fought by every means possible. Jews were linked both to international capitalist conspiracies, which had kept Germany economically weak in the 1920s, and to the rise of the Bolshevik menace in the east, which Germany would have to combat sooner or later. Thus a struggle for living space with Bolshevik Russia, which seemed to Hitler to be inevitable at some point in the future, would also have the virtue of continuing the life-or-death struggle against the Jew.

Hitler's ideas were certainly extreme, but they were not particularly new. Many of his beliefs had been common currency amongst pan-German groups in Vienna and in Munich at the turn of the century, and the aim of German territorial expansion eastwards had been firmly on the agenda of the German high command in the First World War. What Hitler managed to do, however, was to distil his thinking into a few recognizable themes outlined in *Mein Kampf* and in subsequent Party publications, which could be endlessly repeated, and then to identify new and persuasive ways of putting his message across. Hitler made his mark by his skilful use of propaganda, by brilliant visual displays, by the selective use of violence and most strongly by his own phenomenal powers of oratory, discovered by his army employers in the early 1920s. Hitler could captivate, inspire and enthral an audience like no other German leader of the inter-war period, and the economic crisis in Germany from 1929 onwards gave him his opportunity. He took it firmly with both hands.

The consolidation of the Nazi regime

The nationalist leaders who had worked so hard to persuade Hindenburg to install Hitler as German Chancellor calculated that once in office the rabble-rouser would settle down to become a more orthodox political leader. They assumed that his violent and extreme Nazi followers would be disarmed and put under police control. They gambled on the responsibilities of office serving to moderate the extreme views and policies which had brought him to power, and on pressurizing him to seek compromise with the more traditional right-wing nationalists in the Cabinet. In fact, quite the reverse happened, as Hitler's first six hectic months in power soon revealed. The winners of the early internal power struggles were not the nationalist leaders but rather Hitler.

He immediately called for new Reichstag elections and secured a 44 per cent Nazi vote by a combination of propaganda, intimidation and violence, using the full state apparatus to great effect to whip up maximum support throughout Germany. In the course of the election campaign, the Reichstag, the headquarters of the German parliament, was destroyed by a fire which Hitler immediately declared to have been the first stage of a communist conspiracy to overthrow the government and to turn Germany into a communist state. In fact, there is no evidence to support this contention, and rumour circulated at the time that it was the work of Nazi agents out to discredit the communists. More recently, there has been speculation that the Dutch anarchist arrested on the premises at the time was working completely on his own. Whatever the true explanation, the fire gave Hitler and the Nazis the opportunity to pose as the saviours of Germany against the Red Peril. Hitler prevailed upon Hindenburg to issue an emergency decree suspending basic rights for the duration of the emergency, and this decree was never revoked. It was turned first against the communists, and then against the other political parties in turn. The new Reichstag passed an enabling act which allowed Hitler and his government to dispense with constitutional forms and limitations for four years in order to deal with the country's problems. At the same time, within the different states of Germany, Reich commissioners were installed to 'maintain order' and purge 'unreliable elements' from public services and particularly from the police force. By the summer of 1933, all political parties in Germany had been dissolved or eliminated, leaving the Nazis as the only legal party. Moves were initiated to purge the civil service in such a way as to ensure that its members were politically reliable and of pure Aryan stock, untainted by Semitic blood. As he prepared for retirement from his post in Berlin in the summer of 1933, the British

21

Ambassador to Germany, Sir Horace Rumbold, left the British government in no doubt as to what was happening in Germany. He pointed to the 'whirlwind development of Hitler's internal policy' which was causing great uneasiness and apprehension in diplomatic circles. 'I have the impression', he continued, 'that the persons directing the policy of the Hitler government are not normal. Many of us, indeed, have a feeling that we are living in a country where fanatics, hooligans and eccentrics have got the upper hand, and there is certainly an element of hysteria in the policies and actions of the Hitler regime.'

The British government watched uneasily as the whirlwind continued. Within a year of Hitler's appointment, the powers of the Länder or individual German states had been destroyed, the Reichstag had ceased to operate except as a stage for the Nazi Party, and trade unions were being absorbed into a new single national workers' organization, called the National Labour Front. When Hindenburg died in summer 1934, Hitler took over as President, and henceforth all members of the German armed forces had to swear an oath of personal loyalty to him. Concentration camps such as Dachau had already been set up in the spring of 1933 to deal with the political enemies of the Reich, and it was not long before their numbers expanded to deal with Jews, Gypsies, homosexuals, Jehovah's Witnesses, habitual criminals and others whose 'negative' characteristics might obstruct the German rise to greatness. In 1935, a law was proclaimed 'for the protection of German blood and honour' since the 'purity of the German blood is a pre-requisite for the continued existence of the German people'. As a result of this law, Germans of pure Aryan descent were forbidden to marry or have sexual relations with Jews, and were discouraged from marrying non-Aryans. At the same time, it was declared that only those of Aryan blood could be German citizens with full political rights.

Though the extent and implications of Hitler's domestic revolution in Germany were not always fully appreciated or understood abroad, it was abundantly clear that, far from being tamed, Hitler was firmly in control of events and was imposing Nazi doctrines in every sphere of German life. At the same time, however, he was a democratically elected leader who was bringing new hope and renewed self-respect to the German population. Unemployment started to fall and continued its downward trend as Hitler inaugurated vast schemes of public works, especially the construction of public buildings and motorways. Germany was once more a force to be reckoned with in the world as Hitler made it clear that he would not be pushed around by other European leaders and that, if they could not come to an agreement with him about their own disarmament, Germany would start to rearm, illegally if necessary. So along with stories of violence and political repression came reports of Hitler's popularity and of the strength of his political position, a position which became unassailable after the suppression of Ernst Roehm and his supporters in June 1934.

While Hitler recognized the need for a personal armed bodyguard (known as the SS) and for an organized force of tough Nazi stormtroopers (the SA), he was not prepared to allow these paramilitary forces to challenge the position of the regular army whose strength and support he needed for both internal security and expansion abroad. As a showdown approached between the ambitions of the leader of the SA, restless Roehm, backed by nearly a million followers, and the jealously guarded power of the traditional army leadership, Hitler colluded with the army to eliminate the threat from Roehm. In a night of violence and murder, referred to subsequently as the Night of the Long Knives, Roehm and a number of his supporters were brutally killed, along with political rivals or untrustworthy associates whom Hitler wished to remove. There was no doubt after 30 June 1934 that Hitler was master in Germany. To some outside observers, it appeared that Hitler had liquidated the revolutionary wing of his party and was settling down to work through more traditional elites. But at least one foreign leader appreciated the significance of the event and the ruthlessness of its execution. While, in September 1934, Stalin took Russia into the League of Nations (the new international organization established as part of the Paris peace settlement of 1919, and which had met regularly at Geneva since then) and began to formulate the doctrine of popular fronts against Fascism, he also began cagily to weigh up the possibility of coming to some sort of deal with Hitler if mutual interests could be identified.

Early diplomacy and the challenge of German rearmament, 1933–5

Stalin was not the only leader to feel equivocal about the rapid consolidation of Hitler's domestic position. Mussolini was flattered by Hitler's deferential attitude towards the older Fascist leader, and by his identification of German Nazi doctrines with the tenets of Italian Fascism. At the same time, he found Nazi racial doctrines absurd, and was disturbed at the prospect of unrestrained German territorial expansion. Mussolini therefore suggested, in March 1933, a four-power pact between Britain, France, Germany and Italy to begin revision of the 1919 treaties, in the interests of peace.

Hitler's arrival in power, and Mussolini's proposal, confirmed the worst fears of French leaders. Traditional Prussian militarism was being harnessed to aggressive Fascist doctrines, and the result was bound to increase German strength which would be turned sooner or later against France. The French government managed to take the sting out of Mussolini's proposal by insisting that treaty revision could take place only in accordance with League procedures, especially Article 19 which laid down that the League Assembly could advise reconsideration of 'treaties which have become inapplicable' by League Council members, but that the agreement of all – including France – was necessary before changes could take place. At the same time, French air intelligence was reporting that, by the summer of 1933, Germany's legally non-existent air force would be in excess of a thousand planes, a third of them modern bombers. Later the same year, Germany's own statistics revealed that arms expenditure in 1934 would be 40 per cent higher than in the previous two years, and that the percentage of the German budget devoted to military affairs would rise from 10.5 per cent to 21 per cent.

Rapid German rearmament was indeed Hitler's first priority, as he told a Cabinet meeting on 8 February, within ten days of becoming Chancellor. In the early stages, this rearmament was to encompass a massive expansion of the army, far beyond the size of 100,000 specified in the Treaty of Versailles, and a modern air force of bombers and fighters, which was forbidden to Germany under the peace treaties. In talks with army leaders, there was general agreement that, to enable Germany to re-establish its position as a major European power, it needed to be armed to a level which would 'at least afford the chance of success in a war on two fronts, against France and Poland'. Thus, by 1936, army leaders were planning for a peace-time army of about 700,000, and a larger wartime army than in 1914, of nearly 3 million. While this expansion was under way, the new air force was seen as a vital weapon of deterrence against possible intervention by Germany's enemies, especially France. The calculation was that if neighbouring powers knew that Germany was building up a powerful air force, they would be less inclined to risk a preventive strike against Germany in these early vulnerable years when the latter's military power was still considerably less than that of the allied powers. Thus, by the end of 1933, there were already two million German workers engaged in airfield and aircraft factory construction, and by early 1934 there were sixteen thousand workers in the aircraft industry, a total which nearly quadrupled in the following year. The first air force programme of 1933 envisaged ten bomber, seven reconnaissance and seven fighter squadrons, and by August of 1933 an increase had been agreed for a further 29 combat units to be brought in by October 1935. By the end of 1934, the industry had equipped 270 bombers, 99 fighters and 303 reconnaissance aircraft, and Germany also possessed 1,300 machines for training purposes. Clearly, rearmament on such a scale could not be concealed and was bound to alarm the other leading powers of Europe, as Hitler knew full well. But he also appreciated that the League of Nations Disarmament Conference, which convened in 1932, had failed thus far to find a solution to Germany's grievances arising over the failure to materialize of the disarmament pledges agreed by the allied powers in the Treaty of Versailles.

The military section of the Treaty of Versailles, which limited the German army to one hundred thousand, restricted a future German navy to six battleships, six light cruisers and 12 destroyers, and forbade the possession of an air force, had a crucial preamble: Germany was to be disarmed 'in order to render possible the initiation of a general limitation of the armaments of all nations'. But such general limitation had proved almost impossible to achieve during the 1920s. There was some progress on naval limitation between Britain, the United States, Japan, France and Italy at the Washington naval conference of 1922 and the London conference of 1930. But attempts to draw up a draft arms limitation convention agreeable to the major world powers and to members of the League failed completely. A preparatory disarmament commission met at Geneva from 1926 and took five years to compile a draft agreement which could be discussed by government representatives. The scheme was examined in detail in sessions of the League of Nations Disarmament Conference, which met from 1932 to 1934, but agreement could not be reached on ways of assessing fighting capacity or on the basis on which armies should be limited. In view of the failure of other powers to implement measures of arms limitation, German representatives demanded the right to rearm, and began to insist more and more forcibly after January 1933 that, if this right was not secured through negotiations, the German government was prepared to flout the provisions of the Treaty of Versailles and take action to build up the country's armed forces.

There was some sympathy for the German case in Britain. Whereas the British government had reduced spending on the armed forces quite significantly in the 1920s, France and its eastern allies had consistently refused to follow suit. The British government did not think it reasonable for Germany to be surrounded by countries, such as France, Poland and Czechoslovakia, which possessed sizeable armies, while Germany itself should remain restricted to an army of 100,000. If attempts to bring about general arms reductions failed, it was inevitable that Germany would argue strongly for a revision of the Treaty of Versailles to allow it to increase the size of its own armed forces.

The British government shared the concerns of France over the mounting evidence in the course of 1933 of substantial German rearmament, but laid some of the blame for it on French intransigence. If only the French government had cooperated during the 1920s and early 1930s with the British government in meeting legitimate German grievances, Hitler might never have come to power. As it was, a compromise on arms limitation needed to be sought with him as a matter of urgency, before he took the law into his own hands. Ironically, just as Hitler began his programme of illegal rearmament, Britain's armed forces reached their lowest point of the inter-war period, with army numbers at around 180,000 and the navy strictly limited by the treaties of Washington and London. As we shall see in the next section, Japan's invasion of Manchuria in 1931 and menacing attitude to British interests in Shanghai on the Chinese mainland in 1932 had caused great concern to the British government in respect of the navy's continuing ability to protect imperial possessions in the Pacific area. The addition of a German military threat to the status quo in Europe underlined Britain's vulnerability. While a rearmament programme slowly got under way in Britain from 1934 onwards, it would be some time before it could become effective, and meanwhile strenuous efforts must be made to come to an agreement with Germany about levels of armaments and also, it was hoped, peaceful revision of frontiers.

The French government was considering containment of Germany rather than conciliation, but, while the French army was more than double the size of the British and could be swelled to near the million mark by calling up reservists, military planning was geared firmly to defence. The nation's military energies were being consumed by the construction across the northern part of Lorraine of the Maginot line, behind which French troops would mass to halt any future German offensive. The calculation, based on the experience of the First World War, was that France would win the resulting war of attrition only with British and American help. It was therefore important to try to work as closely as possible at least with the British government without compromising on vital French interests. But the British government disapproved of France's alliances with Poland and Czechoslovakia, and was determined to keep its own options open in eastern Europe and to minimize any commitments to countries in that part of the continent. Furthermore, Britain had only skeletal home forces at its disposal to send to France, and then only if the requirements of imperial defence allowed them to be spared. To add to France's problems, the Maginot line so far covered only Lorraine, and left France open to attack through Belgium. While France and Belgium had concluded a treaty in 1920, its existence had caused so much friction within Belgium between the French-orientated Walloons and the more hostile Flemings in the north that very little military planning had actually taken place between the two countries. Similarly, there had been no detailed discussions with east European allies about the implementation of mutual assistance in the event of German aggression. If the French strategy in the event of German attack was to staff the barricades behind the Maginot line, what sort of help would the French army be able to offer if Poland or Czechoslovakia became the first object of attack? No plans existed for lightning attacks on Rhineland bridgeheads, or dashing offensives to divert part of the German army. Here was a serious gap in French military planning which made the construction of eastern pacts by the French government far from easy.

While Britain was therefore pressing for an arms limitation agreement with Germany and trying to pressurize France into making substantial concessions, France was preoccupied with the construction of an east European agreement along the lines of the Locarno Treaty of 1925, which would include Germany. Failing that, the creation of a pact consisting of its east European allies plus Russia and Italy was favoured as a means of containing Germany. The British government supported the eastern 'Locarno' idea, to guarantee by mutual agreement frontiers in eastern Europe as they had been guaranteed in 1925 in western Europe through agreements between France, Belgium, Germany, Italy and Britain. However, if Germany's agreement could not be secured, the British government feared the construction of a bloc of states encircling Germany. British leaders warned that such encirclement might drive Hitler to some desperate act of aggression. But, without British cooperation on measures of security, the French refused to agree to further concessions on arms limitation. Seizing his opportunity, on 14 October 1933, Hitler withdrew the German delegation from the League Disarmament Conference, denouncing it as a sham, and announced Germany's intention to withdraw from the League. However, he added that he would consider returning to Geneva when Germany's grievances were recognized and serious proposals were put forward to meet them.

There was worse news to come. In January 1934, Poland, fearing that treaty revision would be concluded at its expense in some agreement between France and Germany, became the first country to conclude a non-aggression pact with Germany. It would run in the first instance for ten years. Clearly, the news of German rearmament was having its effect on the political calculations of east European leaders. The implementation of Nazi policies in Germany, and Hitler's obvious intention to build up a more powerful German state, also had a galvanizing effect on German communities throughout central and eastern Europe. In the summer of 1934, Nazis in Austria, clamouring for union with their brothers in Germany, were responsible for the murder of the Austrian Chancellor, Engelbert Dollfuss, in an attempt to bring about the desired *Anschluss*.

Would the leading powers of Europe acquiesce in such forceful treaty revision? Neither Britain nor France had any bilateral agreements with Austria, though as fellow League members they were pledged to uphold its political independence and territorial integrity. The major League power which possessed a common frontier with Austria was Italy and, while Hitler hesitated, Mussolini acted decisively in marching his troops to the Brenner pass, the main access route from the south into Austria. Mussolini thus made it very clear to Hitler that he was not prepared to see German power expanded so dramatically and so menacingly in Italy's direction, and his action enabled the Austrian authorities to stabilize the internal situation and, for the moment at least, to crush the Nazi threat. Would Mussolini be prepared to go further and conclude some sort of political pact or military agreement with France and its eastern European allies? One obstacle would be Italy's increasingly close relations with Hungary, and hostility towards Yugoslavia, which was one of France's eastern European associates. Another would be Mussolini's ideological aversion to the closer relations with Russia which France wished to establish. And, as we shall see in the next section, Mussolini had his own territorial ambitions in the Mediterranean region and in North Africa. Would France support Italian expansion in Albania or in Africa?

Despite the difficulties, French leaders and especially the Foreign Minister, Louis Barthou, worked hard during the summer and autumn of 1934 to construct political and military agreements which would include both Russia and Italy, and could serve to contain growing German power. While preliminary talks were held with the Italians, the French found it necessary to soothe Yugoslav fears and try to promote better relations between Yugoslavia and Italy. In order to further this strategy, the King of Yugoslavia was invited to visit France in October 1934. As he arrived in Marseilles, both he and Barthou were struck down by the bullets of a Croatian terrorist. Barthou's successor, Pierre Laval, did not allow rumours of Italian complicity in Croatian terrorist activities to deter him from the pursuit of Italian friendship. In January 1935, Laval visited Mussolini in Rome and concluded a number of agreements covering colonial and continental matters. In return for a free hand to expand Italian interests in Abyssinia, Mussolini was prepared to help construct a Danubian pact and to continue to safeguard Austrian independence. Prospects seemed bright for closer military collaboration, especially for the use by France of air bases in Italy to enable it to assist its east European allies in any future crisis.

The Saar plebiscite, which took place in January 1935, clearly underlined the need for France and Italy to work together to contain German strength. The Treaty of Versailles had stipulated that the Saar could be transferred from League supervision to German rule after fifteen years, if this was the wish of the native inhabitants of the region. The Saarlanders voted in overwhelming numbers to be incorporated into Germany, rather than to be included in France or to continue to be supervised by the League. While the voting, supervised by forces under the control of the League, was conducted in a relatively orderly manner, Nazi propaganda was at its most strident, and Hitler's tirades about the growing strength of Germany were full of menace. It was becoming abundantly clear to France, Italy and Britain by 1935 that German rearmament was proceeding apace, and that, in particular, Germany was constructing a sizeable air force. Far from concealing this development, Hitler took every opportunity to allude to it, hinting all the while that he was willing to discuss arms limitation if other European powers would do the same.

The British Prime Minister Stanley Baldwin had already warned the British people that the country's frontier was now on the Rhine as far as European defence was concerned, and that 'the bomber will always get through'. At the same time, he had assured the House of Commons that Britain's air strength was based on a calculation of at least parity with the strongest air force in Europe. Information coming out of Germany seemed to suggest that the German air force was rapidly overtaking the strength of its British counterpart both in quality and in quantity, and that further expansion was planned. After talks with Laval, the British government decided to accept an invitation from Hitler for Foreign Secretary Sir John Simon and his under-secretary Anthony Eden to visit Berlin to discuss the possibility of concluding an air pact and reaching agreement on other modifications of the Treaty of Versailles. But the visit was postponed by the Germans after the publication of the British White Paper of 1 March 1935, which proposed an increase in service estimates of £10 million, and was justified by references to the 'feeling of insecurity' which had been recently generated in Europe. Goebbels, one of Hitler's closest political colleagues, did nothing to dispel this sense of insecurity when he revealed to the foreign correspondent of the *Daily Mail* on 9 March the establishment of a German military air force under a special ministry. A week later, the Germans announced the reintroduction of universal military conscription to enable thirty-six army divisions totalling about 500,000 men to be raised. The news came a day after the French government had extended its own period of compulsory military service to two years. Ten days later, Simon and Eden were received in Berlin, and Hitler floated the possibility of an air- or naval-limitation agreement with Britain, after boasting that his Luftwaffe had already reached parity with the Royal Air Force.

Germany was thus openly admitting to policies of rearmament in flagrant contravention of the Treaty of Versailles. Furthermore, it was becoming clear to the outside world that these policies were well advanced and were designed to strengthen Germany's demands for further treaty modifications, which it might try to secure by force if they could not be peacefully negotiated. Fully recognizing the challenge and the long-term threat it posed, Britain, France and Italy met together at Stresa in mid-April and condemned the measures of German rearmament which had taken place. They stressed their belief in Austrian independence, pledged themselves to uphold the Locarno agreements, including the continued demilitarization of the Rhineland, and expressed opposition to unilateral treaty violations of the sort which could endanger the peace of Europe. But three developments now occurred, which split open this united front and enabled Hitler to benefit from the resulting tensions. The first was the treaty concluded by France with Russia in mid-May 1935, the second was the naval agreement reached between Britain and Germany in June, and the third and most serious was Mussolini's long-cherished scheme for Italian expansion into Abyssinia, planned for the autumn.

As we have seen, the French Foreign Minister Barthou had hoped to establish closer links with Russia in addition to improving relations with Italy. Poland's pact with Germany, and Germany's growing military strength, underlined the importance of attempting to line Russia up alongside Britain and Italy. Russian entry into the League of Nations in September 1934 promised to mark the first stage of this process. Barthou's successor Laval, however, was not so keen to conclude a full-blown military convention or mutual assistance pact with the Bolshevik government. Quite apart from the tensions it would cause with other east European states, it could have serious domestic political repercussions which might weaken the French government's electoral support. Laval visited Moscow in mid-May 1935. He returned with a mutual assistance pact which was designed to operate only within the framework of the League and the Locarno agreements, and with the promise of a parallel pact entailing a Soviet guarantee to Czechoslovakia. Even this formula worried the British government, raising as it did fears that the only

31

beneficiary of an armed struggle against Hitler would be Bolshevik Russia. Mussolini remained hostile to cooperation with a communist state, and substantial sections of the Italian population and of the British public were more attracted to the prospect of Hitler's crusade against communism than they were to the idea of communist help to contain Hitler.

If France's flirtation with Russia upset Britain and Italy, Britain's naval talks and subsequent naval agreement with Germany deeply offended the French and Italian governments. While in Berlin, Simon had invited a German delegation to come to London to explore with British officials and ministers the possibility of reaching an agreement on limitation of their respective naval strengths. The hostility of many British politicians and civil servants towards the Franco-Russian alliance increased their desire to come to an agreement with Germany as a warning to France against the pursuit of blatant policies of encirclement aimed at Germany. But it was the Far Eastern situation which was the main factor pushing the British government towards a naval agreement with Germany. Britain's naval strength was already fully stretched in maintaining its existing commitments. It was known that Japan was unhappy with the naval restrictions placed upon it by the Treaties of Washington and London, and wished to renegotiate the terms. This could spark off a new naval race with Japan at a time when it was feared that Hitler would also begin to build up his naval strength. Leading members of the Cabinet, and particularly the Chancellor of the Exchequer Neville Chamberlain, were not slow to draw attention to the enormous strain which would be placed on the Treasury if a new armaments race was unleashed. Hitler, meanwhile, placing priority at this stage on building up the strength of his army and air force, offered to limit the German fleet to 35 per cent of each category of the British surface fleet and 45 per cent of the submarine fleet, which would give the British navy a superiority over Germany twice as great as in 1914, and enable it to deal with a crisis in the Far East without the fear of a German strike in the North Sea. Dominion leaders visiting London for the Jubilee celebrations of King George V were not slow to impress upon government ministers the importance of a naval treaty which could both minimize the German naval threat and help to contain a possible Japanese menace.

Accordingly, naval discussions began in London between the two powers on 4 June, and the outlines of an agreement were ratified by the Cabinet a week later. Though the French and Italian governments registered their objections, the British government pressed ahead and concluded the agreement on 18 June. In their closing statements, Hoare and von Ribbentrop declared on behalf of their respective governments that the agreement was designed to facilitate a general treaty on armaments, especially naval forces. Whilst such an agreement may well have been militarily desirable from a British point of view, it was politically inept to say the least. It drove a wedge between Britain on the one hand and the French and Italians on the other, at a crucial time when it was vitally important for the three powers to work together. The British government could claim that it was possible to do business with Nazi Germany in the field of arms limitation. But they had, in the process, condoned German violations of the Treaty of Versailles by agreeing to a German navy considerably in excess of that stipulated by the treaty, and they had not attempted to secure the prior agreement of the other major signatories, France and Italy. What was now to stop Hitler repudiating other provisions of the treaty, fortified by the knowledge that the British government was, if not tacitly supporting him, most unlikely to offer strenuous opposition?

The challenge of Japanese and Italian territorial expansion

The dilemma facing the British government was that by the mid-1930s, as we have seen, Germany was not the only potential threat to British naval supremacy. In the Far East, Japanese expansionist ambitions were gathering alarming pace, whilst in Italy, Mussolini was harbouring plans to extend Italian power around the Mediterranean region and in north-east Africa. Britain was thus confronted with simultaneous threats to its global supremacy in three strategically sensitive areas. Growing Japanese naval and military power threatened British commercial concessions on the Chinese mainland, Hong Kong and, possibly in the future, the dominions of Australia and New Zealand and the naval base at Singapore. A belligerent Italy could obstruct the passage of British ships through the main imperial artery of the Mediterranean Sea, on their way to India and the Far East. And a resurgent Germany revived fears of continental domination which would give Germany mastery of the Low Countries and a springboard for the bombing or invasion of Britain. Thus whilst the British

33

government recognized the growing threat posed by Nazi German rearmament, its response was shaped by global considerations, and not solely by the situation in Europe.

Japan had followed a course of territorial expansion in east Asia since the late nineteenth century. An alliance with Britain, concluded in 1902 and renewed in 1911, had established cordial relations between the two countries, and Japan had entered the First World War on the allied side. But it was very clear from its wartime activities, in taking over German Chinese concessions and possessions in the Pacific, and in imposing the notorious Twenty-One Demands in 1915 on a weak Chinese government, that Japan was using the alliance with Britain to expand its economic and strategic power in China and in the Pacific region. At the Paris Peace Conference in 1919, Japan was for the first time recognized as a great power, with a permanent seat on the Council of the new League of Nations. But its demands for permanent concessions and extended rights in Shantung province in China, and in Manchuria, caused consternation in the United States, and strong American pressure forced Japan to pull out of Shantung in 1922. At the same time, the United States made it clear to the British government that if Britain desired a naval arms limitation agreement between the two countries, which might be extended to cover other naval powers such as Japan, France and Italy, then the Anglo-Japanese alliance would have to be terminated.

Thus in 1922, the Washington Naval Treaty, limiting large capital ships, was concluded between the United States, Britain, Japan, France and Italy. The Anglo-Japanese alliance was replaced by a much looser US–British–Japanese–French four-power agreement to respect each other's possessions and territories in the Pacific region, and the United States, Britain and France agreed not to increase their naval fortifications in the western Pacific area, thus ruling out any strengthening of their bases at Manila, Guam or Hong Kong. While it seemed on the surface, therefore, that Japanese expansionist ambitions had been contained, strong nationalist and imperialist passions remained, particularly centred on the armed forces.

An important concession which Japan had been granted in 1905, after its victory in the war against Russia, was the right to station soldiers in Manchuria to guard the strategic rail network which ran through the province. By the 1920s, this army in Manchuria was observing the disintegration of China as a series of warlords sought

34

to establish and to maximize their spheres of influence in the north and central provinces. Japanese commanders were increasingly drawn into Manchurian politics, as they sought to keep north China weak. And, while the Japanese government worked cooperatively in the 1920s with other powers in the League of Nations, army and navy leaders grew increasingly scornful of what they saw as Japanese politicians kowtowing to western governments and failing to safeguard vital national interests. Passions finally boiled over when, in 1930, the Japanese government concluded with Britain and America the naval treaty of London, which limited the numbers of cruisers which each of the powers could have, to a ratio of ten, ten, and seven (for Japan). Though the Japanese government finally managed to ratify the treaty, army and navy leaders and ultra-nationalist groups whipped up a frenzied campaign against the treaty, which then escalated into wide-scale attacks against political parties, government leaders and anyone who dared to express support for the naval treaty. And in the midst of the agitation, the army in Manchuria seized the opportunity they had been waiting for, to stage an 'incident' in the Mukden region.

Claiming that a bomb had been placed on the railway line at Mukden, Japanese troops stationed in Manchuria fanned out of the railway zones to occupy the whole of south Manchuria. The Chinese government appealed to the League of Nations to intervene and to order the Japanese troops back to their former positions, but, while the Japanese government was formally cooperative at Geneva, the army in Manchuria continued its seizure of territory, until it had occupied the whole of the Manchurian province. A League of Nations enquiry team, led by the British peer Lord Lytton, was despatched to the Far East on a fact-finding mission. Its report, which blamed China as well as Japan for disrupting trade and contributing to instability in the region, called on Japanese troops to withdraw back to their railway-zone bases.

But by this time, in late 1932, the Japanese army in Manchuria had declared the independence of the province as the new state of Manchukuo, claiming local support for the move. The more the League of Nations tried to put pressure on the Japanese government to repudiate what the Manchurian army was doing, the easier it became for ultra-nationalist and militarist supporters to generate mass support within Japan for the army takeover of Manchuria. One reason for this was that, by late 1932, the Japanese population was facing the same severe deflationary pressures as people in Germany were.

A slump in world trade had caused a very sharp drop in Japanese exports, which fell 43 per cent in value between 1929 and 1931. Japanese farmers who produced silk for United States markets suffered particularly large losses, and the resulting distress, which badly affected rural communities, fuelled rising nationalist protests. Pressure mounted on the Japanese government to pull out of international agreements and to take unilateral action to safeguard national economic, strategic and military interests.

To maintain the momentum, ultra-nationalist groups and individual army officers plotted coups against the government, and carried out a number of assassination attacks on government ministers and officials suspected of being western or liberal in out-look. Concerted action by the League of Nations and the United States in the Pacific region might have served to check the agitation, but it proved impossible for Britain and France, the two leading League powers, to coordinate a forceful response to the crisis that the United States was willing to support. A show of combined Anglo-American naval strength in the Pacific might have had a salutary effect on Japanese militarists and nationalists. But, instead, Japanese leaders saw the western powers bitterly divided in their response to the Manchurian crisis, and Britain in particular weakened by the domestic impact of the Great Depression, and by a decade of naval disarmament. Thus inflamed nationalist pressures in Japan were directed to vigorously opposing the League's condemnation of Japanese military actions in Manchuria, and to denouncing the organization. In March 1933, the Japanese government announced that it was withdrawing from the League.

The repercussions of the Manchuria crisis were extremely serious for the British and French governments and for the prospects of international stability. The League of Nations had proved itself to be impotent to deal with conflict in the Far East, in the absence of cooperation from the two great powers in the region, the United States and Russia, and thus its credibility as a peace-keeping organization had been seriously affected. While France's strategic priorities were centred on Europe rather than on its empire, Britain's commercial and strategic interests in the Pacific region, and its base in India, were now threatened by a weak and disunited China and an aggressive Japan.

The crisis had revealed how difficult it would be for Britain to rely on American cooperation or assistance in the Far East, yet at the same time it had exposed the growing territorial and imperial ambitions of the Japanese military. By the end of 1933, Japanese troops had strengthened their hold over Manchuria, and had negotiated a truce with local warlords which created a demilitarized zone thirty miles to the south of the Great Wall of China. How long would it be before they penetrated further south, and set up a 'protectorate' over parts of northern China, or launched a full-scale invasion of China itself? The Manchurian crisis had revealed the militant independence of the Japanese Manchurian army, and their allegiance, not to the Japanese government but to the emperor and to their fanatical version of Japanese traditions. Sooner or later they were likely to expand their territorial base on the Chinese mainland, and to pose a serious, possibly mortal, threat to Britain's extensive commercial and strategic interests in Shanghai and Hong Kong.

Meanwhile, in the Mediterranean region, Mussolini's growing ambitions were also causing concern. Since his accession to power in 1922, the Fascist leader had made no secret of his ambition to raise Italy's status as a European power by increasing its influence around the Mediterranean and by expanding its empire. Unlike Japan, however, Mussolini lacked a strong economic base and well-equipped, effective military forces, and the onset of the Depression made it even harder for him to secure them. Thus he aimed in the short term to seek glorious expansion on the cheap, possibly in Africa at the expense of Abyssinia, but for that he needed the agreement, or at least tacit consent, of Britain and France.

As we have already seen in the previous section, Mussolini was very concerned by the growing evidence of German expansionist aims. He feared the prospect of a dominant Germany pursuing its economic and political interests in eastern and south-eastern Europe at Italy's expense, and threatening his own expansionist ambitions. Now would be the time for Italy to establish its own empire as a clear indication to Germany that, while the Italian Fascist government sympathized with many of the objectives of the German Nazi government, it nonetheless intended to act vigorously to protect and to extend its own Mediterranean and south-east European interests. But what would be the reaction of the British and French governments to Italian colonial expansion? Would they accept it in return for Mussolini's support for pacts to contain Hitler?

It was certainly the case that the two governments had acquiesced in Italian economic penetration of Abyssinia in the 1920s. However, since that time Abyssinia had become a member of the League of Nations, and all other League members were therefore now pledged, under article 10 of the League Covenant, to uphold its political independence and territorial integrity. On the other hand, the British and French governments had not taken the opportunity at the Stresa conference in April 1935 of warning Mussolini of any opposition they might have to his plans. Indeed, in his talks with Mussolini in January, it seems clear that Laval had expressed his support for Italian colonial expansion in Africa in return for Italian support for French policies of German containment in Europe. The problem was, however, that while Laval was no doubt thinking in terms of giving Mussolini a free hand to strengthen Italy's position as the 'protector' of Abyssinia, Mussolini was inclined more and more towards the prospect of a glorious, short, triumphant war of conquest.

Throughout the summer of 1935 it became clear that Italy was massing troops on the Abyssinian border in preparation for a military invasion once the summer rains were over. Would Britain and France now uphold their League of Nations obligations, to the extent of declaring economic or even military sanctions against Italy, in response to its invasion of the territory of a fellow League member, or would they try to broker a deal with Mussolini at the expense of Abyssinian integrity and League credibility? If the declaration of sanctions resulted in war against Italy, would France support Britain in a naval campaign in the Mediterranean Sea, and, if not, what would be the effect of this conflict on Britain's naval position in the Far East, already under threat as a result of Japanese expansion? The British government harboured strong suspicions that Laval would do all he could to minimize League action against Mussolini, and that French naval support could not be relied upon. At the same time, the Cabinet's consideration of policy options was heavily influenced by Prime Minister Baldwin's decision to call a general election in November, 1935. In the course of the campaign, government ministers and supporters worked hard to maximize political support by stressing the government's strong commitment to the League of Nations, at a time when massive support for an independently organized peace ballot had revealed the electorate's widespread support for the League. The British public was led to believe that its government would support the League in taking strong measures against Mussolini, whose troops duly invaded Abyssinia in October 1935.

With the election safely won, however, Sir Samuel Hoare, who had replaced Sir John Simon as Foreign Secretary in June, went to Paris to see whether he could reach agreement with Laval on a package of territorial adjustments and economic concessions which would give Mussolini a large slice of what he wanted in east Africa while still leaving an independent, if somewhat truncated, Abyssinia. The bargain they tentatively struck was immediately leaked in the French press, and reports of this 'Hoare–Laval pact' caused an uproar in Britain. The government was forced to repudiate Hoare's negotiations in Paris, and Hoare himself resigned, to be replaced by Anthony Eden, who was perceived as a strong League supporter. The British government now led the way at Geneva in calling for economic sanctions against Mussolini, and dragged a reluctant French government behind it. But the French would not support oil sanctions, whilst the British were reluctant to agree to the closure of the Suez Canal, both measures which would have caused major problems for the Italian war effort. The French had not abandoned hopes of restoring the Stresa front, and the British did not want to run a serious risk of unleashing a naval war in the Mediterranean – even though British naval commanders there were confident that the outcome would be a British victory. For such a war would threaten vital imperial communications, and Japan would not be slow to exploit the situation to further its own expansionist ambitions in China. So League action was muted, with the result that Italian troops were able to overrun Abyssinia, crush resistance by the use of poison gas amongst other weapons, and proclaim the Italian conquest of a League member state. The League of Nations had suffered its second serious setback in five years, and this time had failed to prevent aggression much nearer to Europe.

Once again, the great powers had shown their inability to work together to resolve serious threats to peace or to protect the interests of weaker League members. These lessons were not lost on Hitler.

The remilitarization of the Rhineland and the Spanish civil war

Far from strengthening Italy's position vis-à-vis Germany, however, Mussolini's colonial expansion resulted in Italy becoming increasingly dependent on German support. It suited Hitler to see the Italians embroiled in African military adventures, and Germany supplied arms to the Abyssinians to prolong the dispute and to sap Italian strength. At the same time, the Abyssinian invasion alienated Italy from Britain and France, and the resulting League condemnation left Italy isolated and needing political help and economic assistance from Germany. And while the attention of the other European powers was concentrated on Mussolini and on Abyssinia, Hitler decided that the time was ripe to remilitarize the Rhineland, in defiance of the clauses in the Treaty of Versailles, repeated in 1925 in the Treaty of Locarno, which stipulated that the Rhineland should be kept free of German troops or military installations. This region was close to the north-eastern border of France, and the French feared that an invasion of France might be launched from the Rhineland.

On 7 March 1936, token German forces, around 10,000 in number, marched into the Rhineland and Hitler announced that the German government was remilitarizing it because of the threat to Germany posed by the Franco-Russian alliance which had just been ratified by the French Senate. Hitler had ordered only a relatively small-scale military operation to carry out the remilitarization, after army leaders had expressed their fears that a larger military exercise would frighten the French into mobilizing their troops and launching a military intervention in the Rhineland. Both Hitler and his army chiefs wanted to avoid armed conflict at this stage, and Hitler gambled that the British and French governments would not oppose a modest German challenge. The gamble paid off, but not because it was unexpected. The move came as no surprise to the French and British governments, both of whom had received a number of prior warnings from their intelligence services and diplomatic staffs. The remilitarization was therefore viewed as a further challenge to the Versailles settlement and to the British government's wish to secure peaceful and orderly revision through agreed negotiation between Europe's leading powers.

The British government had already gone out of its way to indicate to Hitler that ministers were willing to agree to German remilitarization of the Rhineland, but only as part of a more general package of measures which could include an air pact, German return to the League of Nations, some peaceful revision of Germany's eastern frontiers and the return of former German colonies. Now

Hitler showed once again, as in his rearmament policies, that he was not willing to achieve his objectives by participating in lengthy multilateral diplomatic discussions. He preferred the direct approach of the pre-emptive strike, in this case by taking unilateral military action and gambling that there would be no armed response. In any event, there were also considerable numbers of armed police and reserve troops in the Rhineland who could be counted on to engage with any invading forces and resist their advance.

The French government had been less keen than the British to negotiate away the demilitarized status of the Rhineland, which was such an important element in its post-war military security system. However, it had no plans ready to counter pre-emptive German action. Thus it was unprepared to take the military offensive and unwilling to act alone. Unfortunately the Hoare–Laval fiasco and disagreements over oil sanctions against Mussolini had soured relations with both Britain and Italy, making the prospect of a joint military venture with one or both powers most unlikely, as Hitler well knew. The day before the remilitarization, Belgium and France had renounced their treaty of guarantee of 1920. Therefore, despite the fact that the German action violated not just the Treaty of Versailles but also the Treaty of Locarno, freely assented to by Germany in 1925, Hitler could be fairly confident that the response of the Locarno powers, principally France, Britain and Italy, would be muted.

In retrospect, many politicians and commentators have claimed that this was the decisive point at which Hitler should have been challenged, and that, when no action was taken in the spring and summer of 1936 to check his aggression, he could no longer be stopped from an expansionist course which would sooner or later inevitably plunge Europe into a war. However, the perception at the time, particularly in Britain, was rather different. Popular sentiment in both Britain and France was very strong that any action which might lead to hostilities and to war should be avoided. Lord Lothian's comment, that the Germans were, after all, 'only going into their own back garden' was widely supported. The Rhineland remilitarization coincided with the beginning of an election campaign in France, which led to a low-key approach to the crisis by politicians. Germany's violation of its treaty obligations was referred to the League by the French government in the hope that economic sanctions against Germany might be invoked. But though the German action was condemned, no punishment was suggested. Sanctions were still in force against Italy, and many countries were feeling the economic pinch. They did not wish to increase their economic difficulties by cutting off trade with Germany. Some states called for Germany's return to the League, so that differences could be resolved at Geneva. Hitler did not rule this out as a possibility for the future, but meanwhile German troops remained in the Rhineland and began to construct fortifications along the frontier with France, opposite the defensive French installations of the Maginot line.

Why were the British and French governments not prepared to take stronger action against Hitler in 1936, when he had demonstrated so clearly his intention to destroy the Versailles settlement by force if necessary? As I have explained in another Lancaster Pamphlet (*Versailles and After*), the British government had been unhappy about the Versailles settlement from the start, believing it to be harsh and in some respects unjust. It had worked to revise it throughout the 1920s, only to run up against very determined French opposition to any changes. British governments and the British public therefore sympathized to a considerable extent with Hitler's determination to shake off the shackles of Versailles and to establish Germany once again as a leading European power.

This was a development which France had fought strenuously to prevent and then to contain. But it could not contain it alone, and France had been singularly unsuccessful in its attempts to forge close military links with Britain, Italy or Belgium. It had managed to conclude an agreement with Russia, but this only offered the promise of possible military cooperation in the future, while it brought immediate political embarrassment in the shape of strong Polish, Italian and British disapproval. Without the assurance of military support from Britain or Italy, Belgium or an east European ally, France was not prepared to challenge Hitler in 1936.

In both Britain and France, the memory of the devastation of the First World War remained strong. Successive governments were determined to do all they could to avoid being dragged into such a conflict again, and their electorates strongly supported policies geared to defence and, in the French case, to deterrence. In Britain, considerable disarmament had taken place, partly as a result of reductions in the amounts of money allocated to the service departments and partly because of the widespread support for programmes of armament limitation which, it was hoped, would preserve peace. Support for disarmament and for a foreign policy based on the League of Nations came from the churches, from members of all political parties and from many influential newspapers. Unfortunately, by the mid-1930s, a general disarmament convention had not been agreed by League members, and the League had singularly failed to deal with a succession of crises, including Japan's invasion of Manchuria and Italy's war on Abyssinia. Meanwhile, the British navy was facing increasingly serious challenges in the Mediterranean Sea and in the Pacific region. Britain's small army was based in India, and was busy trying to damp down uprisings across the empire, which were growing in areas such as Palestine. Even had the British government considered a military response to German remilitarization of the Rhineland, very few troops were based in Britain for immediate deployment to the European mainland. Not surprisingly, therefore, the British government was keen to employ diplomacy as far as possible rather than military means to deal with Hitler's grievances and thus avoid the danger of being dragged into another war.

Such an approach was dictated also by the attitudes of the United States and the British Dominions. The United States, though it was rapidly becoming the world's leading economic and naval power, was reluctant to become politically or militarily involved either with the League or in Europe. Even in the Pacific region, as we have seen, the United States was not willing to work closely with Britain to contain growing Japanese military and naval power. The overseas British Dominions – Canada, South Africa, Australia, New Zealand – urged successive British governments not to enter into European commitments but to ensure that imperial defence remained their top military and naval priority. Straddled across eastern Europe and Asia there was the enigma of the Soviet Union under Stalin, modernizing and industrializing through a series of five-year plans. Most British government leaders in the 1930s were extremely suspicious of the intentions of the Soviet regime, and were reluctant to work with Stalin or with Bolshevik representatives at Geneva, once the Russian government had joined the League in 1934. Rather than try to court Soviet assistance in attempts to contain German power, as the French government was doing, it seemed to British government leaders to be a safer option to ignore the Soviet Union as a factor in European politics, as far as possible.

It was in this situation that the British government formulated what has become known as a policy of 'appeasement' to deal with

Nazi grievances. In some respects, British governments had pursued policies of appeasement towards Germany since 1919 in working to revise the peace treaties and to restore German political and economic strength. But the process had been controlled by the British government, with Germany very much on the defensive. By the mid-1930s, Britain was in a weaker position to control the process of treaty revision and, as we have seen, under Hitler, Germany took the offensive. British and French governments have been heavily criticized for agreeing to a whole succession of German demands and thus for encouraging Hitler's territorial ambitions. The criticism has been particularly directed at Neville Chamberlain, Prime Minister of Britain from 1937 to 1940, who doggedly pursued a policy of appeasement of German demands even in the face of considerable Nazi provocation and bullying. While some historians have since argued that Chamberlain's acquiescence in Hitler's demands made a European war more likely, the whole basis of Chamberlain's policy was to try to avoid war for as long as possible. He did not want to risk conflict over Nazi territorial claims in central and eastern Europe, which he regarded as a legitimate and traditional area for German ambitions. He was sympathetic to Hitler's desire to unite in one Reich the German-speaking populations of Austria, Czechoslovakia and Poland. He saw such a Reich as a strong barrier to Bolshevik expansion westwards. Furthermore, the creation of a stable European territorial and political settlement, if it could be achieved, would enable Britain to pursue its overseas trading interests and maintain its imperial possessions without the need to enter into any European commitments. But, at the same time, Chamberlain and his Cabinet colleagues did recognize that Britain urgently needed to build up its armed strength, in the face of the mounting challenges to the British Isles and to the far-flung empire. While programmes of rearmament got under way from the mid-1930s, Chamberlain was conscious both of the time they would take to become effective and of their considerable cost. For the time being, therefore, he put all his energies into attempts to negotiate territorial change peacefully both with Hitler and with Mussolini.

Chamberlain's approach did not go unchallenged. Winston Churchill denounced him and his Cabinet colleagues regularly in the House of Commons, and urged the need for a strong system of alliances and for more rapid and extensive rearmament to check Hitler. The French government was sympathetic to Churchill's approach, but did not dare to disagree too strongly with Chamberlain, for fear of losing British support and the hope of British assistance in any future conflict. In any event, Churchill's was a lone voice in calling for measures of resistance against German remilitarization of the Rhineland and against union with Austria. If such measures ran the risk of war, they were strongly opposed in Britain, and even more so if they involved a pact or alliance with Soviet Russia. Even rearmament, which gathered pace in the late 1930s, was accepted only grudgingly as necessary in the event of Hitler pursuing more grandiose ambitions such as the complete domination of Europe. If there were realistic alternatives to the policy of appeasement in the mid- and later 1930s, Chamberlain's contemporaries were very reluctant to outline them or to spell out their implications and urge that they be put into practice. There was very little opposition to the policy of appeasement pursued by the British government until after the Munich agreement in October 1938, and by that time Hitler had built Germany up into a formidable military and territorial power.

The outbreak of the Spanish civil war in the summer of 1936, triggered off by General Franco's challenge to the Spanish republican government, underlined the extent to which the British and French governments had been pushed onto the defensive. In France, Blum's Popular Front coalition of socialists, communists and radicals had just taken office and was struggling to build up French armed strength against a background of severe economic depression. Not only could France not spare cash or armed assistance to help the beleaguered Spanish republican government, but even the serious discussion of such help could spark off considerable political opposition from the Right, especially after Russia began to send arms to the republican side and comintern agents organized international brigades to fight in Spain. Britain had no wish to be dragged into yet another area of conflict and was therefore keen to agree with France on a policy of non-intervention. Meanwhile, Mussolini began to send Italian troops on a considerable scale to assist Franco, and Germany supplied aircraft and pilots and learned a lot about the practicalities of modern aerial warfare. Spain became the battlefield for a European-wide struggle between the forces of communism and socialism on the one hand and the forces of fascism on the other. Britain and France could try to stay out, but the reverberations of the struggle had a profound effect within the two countries and throughout Europe. The war dragged on for three years, but it was clear by early 1937 that Franco was establishing a strong position and that France was in great danger of being menaced by fascist-style governments on three of its frontiers. French problems were compounded by the Belgian government's declaration of a policy of neutrality in late 1936, and by the construction in the Rhineland of a German Siegfried line of fortifications which would cut France off completely in wartime from military contact with its east European allies.

The onward march of fascism was underlined by the anti-comintern pact concluded between Germany and Japan in November 1936, to combat the spread of communist regimes. It was ostensibly directed against the USSR, but the seemingly close relations established between the two governments also posed a serious threat to the British empire. This threat was magnified when Italy adhered to the pact in late 1937. The Spanish civil war and the establishment of the left-wing Popular Front government in France, coming hard on the heels of the Abyssinian adventure had finally pushed Mussolini into Hitler's arms. The result was the formation of a very menacing German–Italian–Japanese combination. In December 1937, the British Chiefs of Staff warned that they could not 'foresee the time when our defence forces will be strong enough to safeguard our trade, territory and vital interests against Germany, Italy and Japan at the same time . . . they could not exaggerate the importance from the point of view of Imperial Defence of any political or international action which could be taken to reduce the number of our potential enemies and to gain the support of potential allies'.

The British Cabinet was acutely aware, however, that the threat of Japanese aggression against British Far Eastern possessions could not be contained by British action alone. It needed to be countered by the United States as well, acting in tandem with Britain, but this seemed increasingly unlikely after the passing of the American Neutrality Act of 1935. Even after Japan launched a full-scale invasion of China in 1937, the United States government showed no signs of wanting to coordinate action with Britain, or to invoke economic or military sanctions against Japan. Indeed, this reluctance to become involved either in the Far East or in Europe made it more imperative for the British government to try to seek agreement with Mussolini or with Hitler, if at all possible. The alternative course of action was massive rearmament, which would be enormously costly and might merely spark off an arms race infinitely more dangerous than the one which took place before 1914 and which was widely perceived to be a major cause of the First World War. But could agreement be reached on terms which would be acceptable to the British government, and would it be kept? Could Hitler and Mussolini be trusted to keep to their word, or were their appetites for expansion increased by every set of attempted negotiations?

Hitler was well aware that Germany's political and military position was improving dramatically in the course of 1936 and 1937, but at the same time the economic strain on Germany was considerable. By the spring of 1936, butter and meat shortages were beginning to appear, along with shortages of vital imports of raw materials and of foreign exchange. The President of the German Reichsbank, Schacht, suggested that the pace of rearmament should be slackened to enable more exports to be produced, and that measures should be taken to devalue the German currency and to expand foreign trade. But Hitler was adamant that foreign trade could not solve Germany's economic and political problems, nor could it guarantee sufficient German military might to crush the growing Bolshevik challenge. His unswerving ideological belief, expressed strongly in a memorandum of August 1936, was that only the acquisition of more living space and agriculturally useful land could do that. He declared that the German army and economy had to be made ready for war within four years, and he accordingly gave Goering wide-ranging powers, through the Four Year Plan pronounced in the summer of 1936, to ensure that this vital state of readiness was reached. In the process, Germany was to make every effort to become more self-supporting by developing a wide range of synthetic materials, by stockpiling essential raw materials and by concluding bilateral trade agreements with states in eastern and south-eastern Europe whereby food and raw materials were supplied to Germany in exchange for manufactured goods and armaments. Romania was a particular target for German advances because it could offer vitally needed supplies of oil.

However, as German rearmament continued at breakneck pace through 1937, crucial shortages in vital materials and human resources threatened to delay implementation of the ambitious targets now being set, not just for the air force and for the army – a peace-time level of 830,000 men, to be expanded to over 4.5 million in war – but also for the navy, where Hitler now ordered ten battleships to be ready by 1944, rather than the previous four. The services were increasingly forced to compete ferociously for supplies of steel and aluminium and for labour, and it was to try to resolve this crisis that Hitler summoned the War Minister, Commanders in Chief of the three services and the Foreign Minister to an urgent meeting in November 1937. It was at this meeting, recorded by Hitler's military adjutant Hossbach, that Hitler emphasized the need for Germany to acquire living space in eastern Europe, by force if necessary. He reiterated his view that 'It is not a case of conquering people but of conquering agriculturally useful space'. Since Germany's 'hateful enemies', who by this stage included Britain, which had resisted his attempts to draw it into closer relations, as well as France, would take measures to stop such German expansion, war would probably result and therefore Germany should plan for action in the near future while these two powers were still militarily weak. The first aim would be 'to conquer Czechoslovakia and Austria simultaneously'. Not all army commanders and officials approved of these objectives or believed that they could be attained without serious military risk to Germany itself. However, dissenters such as the War Minister General Blomberg, head of the army General von Fritsch and Foreign Minister Neurath were ruthlessly removed from power in February 1938, when Hitler decided to appoint himself as Supreme Commander of the German Army.

To the British government, Hitler played upon the desire of Germans throughout eastern Europe to be reunited with the German Reich, a feeling which he could not ignore. He also emphasized his hatred and distrust of communism and of Bolshevik Russian ambitions. Neville Chamberlain, who took over as British Prime Minister from Baldwin in May 1937, sympathized with these feelings. He wrote to one of his sisters, 'Of course they want to dominate eastern Europe. They want as close a union with Austria as they can get, without incorporating her into the Reich, and they want much the same thing for the Sudeten Deutsch as we did for the Uitlanders in the Transvaal'. Chamberlain was not opposed to peaceful revision in eastern Europe, though he knew the French government would try to prevent it. He was willing to try to come to an accommodation with Hitler over arms, east European problems and the possible return of German colonies. At the same time, he continued to support policies of rearmament in Britain, and tried to improve relations with Mussolini, despite Italy's adherence to the anti-comintern pact, and its announcement in December 1937 that it was leaving the League of Nations. In February 1938, Chamberlain came to an agreement with Mussolini, over which the Foreign Secretary, Eden, resigned in protest, that Britain would recognize the Italian conquest of Abyssinia in return for the withdrawal of some 10,000 Italian troops from Spain. A month later, he was confronted with the *Anschluss* crisis.

The *Anschluss* with Austria and the Czechoslovak crisis, 1938

Since 1934, the Austrian government had struggled to keep the Austrian Nazis under control and German influence at bay. But, to be successful, this strategy needed the support of the Italian government, which was lost after 1936. By 1937, Nazi newspapers were circulating freely throughout the major Austrian towns, and two Nazi supporters joined the Austrian Cabinet. The Austrian Chancellor, Schuschnigg, was losing control of the political situation, and Germany's ambassador in Vienna, Papen, suggested that a meeting with Hitler might help to put future relations on a clearer footing. After Hitler's brutal dismissal of Blomberg, Fritsch and Neurath, Schuschnigg was summoned to Hitler's retreat at Berchtesgaden, close to the Austrian border. There he was received by Hitler in a most hostile manner, being bullied and threatened because of his alleged intransigence towards Germany. Hitler hinted that, if Schuschnigg was not more accommodating towards the Austrian Nazis and more agreeable to appointing one of them as Minister of the Interior, he could not be responsible for the consequences. Schuschnigg took the hint, and on his return to Vienna made the requisite appointment, but he also announced that he would hold a plebiscite on 13 March to seek the support of Austrians for a 'free and German, independent and social, Christian and united Austria'. An enraged Hitler immediately demanded its cancellation, and opposition to the move was whipped up amongst Austrian Nazis. When, with the German army mobilized, no help was forthcoming for Austria from Italy, France or Britain, Schuschnigg resigned, and German troops marched into Vienna on 12 March. Hitler returned to his home town of Linz and declared the union

(*Anschluss*) of Austria and Germany to a vast cheering crowd. The German-speaking populations of Innsbruck, Salzburg and Vienna also gave German troops a rapturous welcome and, when Hitler finally drove into the Austrian capital on 14 March, he was given a tumultuous reception, with scenes of enthusiasm, according to one Swiss reporter, which 'defied all description'. All the Catholic church bells in Vienna were ringing, and swastika banners were flying from their steeples. The next day, Hitler addressed a huge cheering crowd of around a quarter of a million people in the city centre who noisily celebrated with Hitler 'the entry of my homeland into the German Reich'. At the same time, the Viennese Nazi Party, reinforced by German SS leaders, was busy rounding up dissidents and Jews; between 10,000 and 20,000 people were arrested and taken into custody in the first stages of the *Anschluss*.

The *Anschluss* was a triumph for Hitler. There had been no foreign intervention and no military or political opposition. At a stroke, Hitler had laid the foundation for his 'Greater Germany', and now further expansion eastwards beckoned. The union of Austria and Germany had stirred up pan-German feelings in neighbouring Czechoslovakia where, in the Sudeten border region, there were heavy concentrations of German-speaking people. Reeling from the shock of *Anschluss*, British and French leaders now had to face demands from Sudeten leaders for the incorporation of all German-speaking Czech subjects into Germany, or for full autonomy within the Czech state. The Czech government refused to entertain their demands, and in May 1938 there were rumours that Germany was ready to attack Czechoslovakia. The Czechs mobilized in readiness, but no German offensive came. The British and French governments breathed again, but Hitler was furious, believing that the failure of the anticipated German military action had made him look foolish in the eyes of other European leaders. He told his chief military and political advisers on 28 May that, when the next crisis arose, the German military response would be suitably impressive and Czechoslovakia would be wiped off the map. The date pencilled in for military action was 1 October 1938.

The British government laboured through the summer to come up with a solution. It suggested that a mediator should be sent to Czechoslovakia to hold talks with the government and with the Sudeten Germans, and to try to find a compromise formula whereby the Germans would achieve some of their demands for greater self-government but within the framework of the existing Czechoslovak state. Lord Runciman travelled to Czechoslovakia on 5 August, but his mission was a failure. The Czech government was willing to make concessions but not to the extent of endangering the unity of the state. After all, apart from its substantial German minority, the state also included large numbers of Slovaks and smaller numbers of Poles and Hungarians. If they all started agitating for independence or for self-rule, there would be no viable Czechoslovak state left. The Sudeten German leader, Henlein, meanwhile, was in constant touch with Berlin and had already defined his tactics to Hitler in the spring: 'We must always demand so much that we can never be satisfied'. The more concessions the British government urged on the Czechoslovak government, the more the Sudeten Germans demanded. And behind them loomed the menacing figure of Hitler, threatening to send in his armies to secure justice for the Sudetens if no solution could be found to their grievances. As Heinlein's colleague, Frank, reported to him at the end of August, whatever concessions were forthcoming to appease Sudeten grievances, the 'Führer is bent on war'.

In Germany itself, 'there is serious unrest on account of the situation', Goebbels noted. 'Everywhere there is talk of war'. Hitler's ruthless determination to invade and to crush Czechoslovakia as soon as possible caused considerable alarm, not only amongst the population at large but also within army and government circles. The army chief of staff, Beck, warned that Britain and France would come to Czechoslovakia's aid, and that Germany would be defeated. The Secretary of State in the German Foreign Office argued that a war would be disastrous not just for Germany but for the whole of European civilization, with the victors being 'the non-European continents and the anti-social powers'. As 1 October, Hitler's declared deadline for attack, approached, an anti-Hitler conspiracy developed which included in its numbers German army officers, diplomats and conservative nationalists. One of their number came to London to try to persuade the British government to declare its intention to intervene militarily if Germany attacked Czechoslovakia. At the annual Nazi Party rally at Nuremberg on 12 September, Hitler demanded self-determination for the Sudeten Germans in a menacing tirade of threats directed against the Czech government. His speech aroused great passions in the Sudeten areas, but the Czech government took immediate steps to declare martial law, and brought the situation under control.

It was at this crucial point in the unfolding crisis that the British Prime Minister, Neville Chamberlain, made his fateful intervention. He was appalled that Europe appeared to be on the brink of yet another armed conflict over the pleas of the Sudeten Germans for self-determination. If Germany invaded Czechoslovakia, France would be bound to assist its east European ally and Russia also had treaty obligations to come to Czechoslovakia's aid. Britain would then be dragged in on France's heels and it would be 1914 all over again. On 13 September, Chamberlain informed the German government that he was willing to go to Germany to discuss the crisis personally with Hitler. Two days later, the sixty-nine-year-old Prime Minister, in his bid to secure European peace, made his very first flight – from Croydon to Munich – and was then transported in Hitler's special train to Berchtesgaden. In the ensuing talks, the two leaders came to an agreement that any districts in Czechslovakia with a German majority which opted for self-determination should be peacefully transferred to the German Reich, and, on his return to England, Chamberlain spent the next week putting pressure on the French and Czech governments to agree to this proposal. When he returned to Germany on 22 September, however, to report his success to Hitler, he was greatly taken aback when a hectoring Hitler presented him with new demands, including an immediate German military occupation of part of Czechoslovakia, plebiscites in additional areas and the satisfaction of Polish and Hungarian claims to Czech-held territory as well as German ones. In despair, Chamberlain protested, 'That's an ultimatum . . . you have not supported in the slightest my efforts to maintain peace'. Just at this point, news arrived that Benes, the Czech leader, had announced the general mobilization of the Czech army. War now seemed inevitable.

But Hitler's tactics had stiffened Chamberlain's resolve, and had changed the mood back in London. In response to the Führer's threats and new demands, Chamberlain and his Cabinet colleagues decided to make it clear to him that, if Germany attacked Czechoslovakia, France and Britain would come to its assistance. At the same time, Chamberlain contacted Mussolini to enlist his support in a bid to persuade Hitler to resume negotiations rather than to resort to force. The Prime Minister's emissary, Sir Horace

Wilson, duly passed on to Hitler in a tense meeting on 27 September Chamberlain's message that 'If in pursuit of her Treaty obligations, France became actively engaged in hostilities against Germany, the United Kingdom would feel obliged to support her'. An infuriated Hitler hit back, 'If France and England strike, let them do so . . . It is Tuesday today, and by next Monday we shall all be at war'.

Hitler's determination to press ahead with a military attack on Czechoslovakia on 1 October if the Czechs did not yield seemed as strong as ever, despite the likelihood of British and French intervention. Yet by the following morning, uncharacteristically, he had changed his mind. He had retreated from an 'unalterable decision', and, as a contemporary noted in his diary, 'One can't grasp this change. Führer has given in, and fundamentally'.

Chamberlain's diplomacy, aimed at exerting the maximum pressure on Hitler to agree to a peaceful settlement, had undoubtedly unnerved and unsettled Hitler. Chamberlain had delivered a radio broadcast to the British people about how absurd it was to be brought to the brink of another European war on account of 'a quarrel in a faraway country between people of whom we know nothing'. He followed this up with a letter to Hitler, expressing his incredulity that the German leader was prepared to risk a war, which might bring the end of civilization, 'for the sake of a few days' delay in settling' the long-standing Sudeten problem. As things stood, the French and British governments were prepared to press the Czechs to cede the Sudeten territory straight away, starting on 1 October, with an International Boundary Commission working out the details of the territorial settlement. The French ambassador in Germany reinforced the message to Hitler. Given that a military conflict with Czechoslovakia was likely to spread and to engulf all of Europe, he argued, why take the risk when nearly all Germany's demands on behalf of the Sudeten Germans could be attained? But it was Mussolini's intervention with Hitler that tipped the balance, and persuaded Hitler to postpone hostilities for twenty-four hours. The Italian ambassador in Germany, Attolico, informed Hitler that Mussolini had been urged by the British government to act as a mediator in the Sudeten crisis. While Mussolini supported Germany, he believed that 'the acceptance of the English proposal would be advantageous' and appealed for a postponement of mobilization. Hitler readily agreed to this suggestion, and a short time later told the British Ambassador, Sir Neville Henderson, that, at the request of his 'great friend and ally, Signor Mussolini', he had postponed mobilization for twenty-four hours.

Thus, on 29 September 1938, Chamberlain, Hitler, Mussolini and the French Prime Minister Daladier, all assembled at the fateful conference at Munich to save the peace of Europe. No Czech representative was present. After thirteen hours of discussions, a compromise solution was hammered out. Germany would occupy specified areas of Czechoslovakia by 1 October, and an international commission would determine a provisional new frontier by 10 October, with German occupation up to that line. War had been averted, but at the cost of forcing Czechoslovakia to cede an important frontier area to Germany, which left it vulnerable to future Polish and Hungarian demands as well as to German military attack. Russia had been quite deliberately excluded from the Munich talks, though it had treaty commitments to Czechoslovakia, and Britain and France had not sought Russia's advice or assistance in any way. France had been unable to guarantee the integrity of its ally, and Daladier was well aware of the sense of shame which many French people felt at this betrayal. Even Chamberlain found the conference a 'prolonged nightmare', but had tried hard to achieve something positive from it. The day after the Munich agreement he had managed to induce Hitler to sign a piece of paper agreeing to settle all matters of mutual interest through consultation which, he declared triumphantly on his return to England, meant 'peace for our time'. He told the British Cabinet on 3 October, 'We were now in a more hopeful position, and . . . the contacts which had been established with the Dictator Powers opened up the possibility that we might be able to reach some agreement with them which would stop the armaments race.'

Relief that war had been avoided was strong not just in Britain, France and Italy but in Germany as well. Goebbels wrote in his diary on 1 October, 'We have all walked on a thin tightrope over a dizzy abyss . . . The word "peace" is on all lips. The world is filled with a frenzy of joy. Germany's prestige has grown enormously. Now we are really a world power again. Now it's a matter of rearm, rearm, rearm . . .'

Hitler, however, felt cheated. He had been spoiling for a fight. But a combination of pressures, including the obvious lack of enthusiasm of the German people themselves for another war, had thwarted his intentions and forced him into international agreements limiting German freedom of manoeuvre and containing eastern expansion. Thus he regarded Munich as a setback to his expansionist ambitions, but only a temporary one. Some weeks later, speaking to an audience of 400 journalists and editors, he outlined his determination, as a matter of urgency, to transform the psychology of the German people and to make them see that 'there are things which *must* be achieved by force if peaceful means fail'. In future, foreign policy issues needed to be presented in such a way that 'the inner voice of the nation itself' gradually began to 'call for the use of force'. So while Chamberlain was cherishing the illusion that the Munich settlement had brought lasting peace, Hitler was already setting a timetable for the next stage of German expansion. On 21 October, he signed a military directive to the effect that the German army, the Wehrmacht, 'must at all times be prepared for the following eventualities: 1. securing the frontiers of the German Reich and protection against surprise air attacks; 2. liquidation of the remainder of the Czech state; 3. the occupation of Memelland'. In the same month, Goering set out a new armaments programme, which envisaged a virtually impossible quintupling of the German air force by 1942, pressing ahead with army expansion and securing a substantial battle fleet through completion of the 'Z plan' by 1943–4.

Thus Chamberlain's hopes of peace did not survive the winter. As soon as the Czech crisis was resolved, the German government started pressurizing the Poles to induce them to agree to the construction by Germany of an extraterritorial road and railway across the Polish corridor, and for the return to Germany of Danzig. The German inhabitants of the Lithuanian port of Memel began to clamour for reunion with Germany. By the beginning of 1939, Hitler stepped up the campaign to bring about the internal dismemberment of Czechoslovakia by encouraging Polish, Hungarian and Slovak claims and by bullying the Slovaks into declaring their independence. On 15 March, German troops invaded the remainder of the Czechoslovak state. A week later, the Lithuanian port of Memel was seized and occupied by German troops.

In Britain, the optimism of October now turned into deep anger at Hitler's cynical disregard of his Munich undertakings. In Parliament and in the country there was a strong groundswell of feeling that Hitler should be stopped before he became master of the entire European continent. Poland appeared to be Hitler's next target, and there were a flurry of reports in January and February of 1939 that a German attack was imminent on one of a range of targets: Memel, Poland, Czechoslovakia or the Ukraine, and in the west, the Netherlands and possibly Switzerland. The British Cabinet now took a step which it had resisted for twenty years. On 31 March, the British government offered a guarantee to Poland that, if it was the victim of an unprovoked attack, Britain would come to its aid. The French government followed suit, and similar guarantees were offered to Romania and, after the Italian invasion of Albania in the second week of April, to Greece as well. But despite the substantial rearmament which had taken place in both Britain and France, there were great logistical problems in making the guarantees effective. How could Britain or France come directly to Poland's aid in the event of a German attack? They could offer arms and financial help, but for how long would Poland be able to fight on its own, while French forces were mobilized behind the Maginot line, and while the British government put together an expeditionary force to fight alongside the French? Only Russia could offer Poland immediate military help, but the Polish government was adamant that no Russian troops would be allowed to enter Polish territory. Russia had not been included in the Munich negotiations, and the French government had made no real attempts since 1935 to strengthen the Franco-Russian pact or to press for joint staff talks. It was known that there had been a severe purge of the Russian armed forces between 1936 and 1938 and, as a result, experts were at best uncertain, and at worst dismissive, about the effectiveness and fighting capacity of the Russian armed forces. On the other hand, because of its crucial geographical position and vast human and mineral resources, Russia could be ignored no longer. Its help against Germany was desperately needed and, consequently, the British and French governments tried to open discussions with Russian diplomats to see what assistance the Soviet government might be prepared to give.

The western powers' unconditional guarantee to Poland, however, had put Russia into a strong bargaining position. Before March, Stalin's reading of the events culminating in the Munich settlement was that Hitler's seemingly inexorable march eastwards was being encouraged by Britain and France in a bid to keep him from seeking conflict in the west and would result, sooner rather than later, in an armed attack on Russia. But now a German attack

56

on Poland would automatically involve Britain and France in military action, giving Russia some freedom for manoeuvre. Russia could afford to press for favourable terms from the British and French governments and could also afford to throw out feelers to Germany about a possible deal. Thus, while Britain proposed that each of the three powers should give separate unilateral guarantees to Poland and Romania, and while France sought a Franco-Soviet treaty binding both to go to the assistance of Poland and Romania, Stalin pitched his demands ever higher, asking for precise military commitments to accompany a three-power treaty of mutual assistance, and demanding freedom for Russia to 'assist' east European states against military attack by sending troops into their territories. Poland, Lithuania, Latvia and Estonia urged the British and French governments not to agree to this demand, and a military mission, which did not arrive in Moscow until mid-August, was threatened with deadlock on the issue. A week later it and the whole of Europe were astounded when Ribbentrop, on behalf of Hitler, and Stalin announced the conclusion of a German–Soviet non-aggression pact.

Since late May, Hitler had been determined 'to attack Poland at the first suitable opportunity . . . Danzig is not the subject of the dispute at all. It is a question of expanding our living space in the East'. But a German seizure of Polish territory would surely bring war this time, even though Hitler was contemptuous of the weakness of the 'little wormlets' he had negotiated with at Munich. Germany would face the risk of attack from two sides, and, although Hitler could hope for Italian support after the conclusion of the Pact of Steel with Mussolini on 22 May, he knew that Italy was hopelessly unprepared for a major war. It was therefore imperative to try to strike a bargain, however temporary, with Stalin over the partition of Poland and the establishment of spheres of influence in eastern Europe. Hitler was confident that such an agreement would frighten Britain and France into backing out of their undertakings to Poland, and he went ahead with plans for the invasion of Poland to take place at the beginning of September.

Negotiations between Germany and the Soviet Union appear to have started in earnest in April 1939, when the Soviet ambassador in Berlin told the permanent head of the German Foreign Ministry, Weiszacker, that there was no reason why relations between the two countries should not be capable of improvement; a month later the Germans moved to reopen negotiations for an economic agreement with Russia which they had tried to initiate with-out success earlier in the year. Discussions took place at a fairly leisurely pace for some weeks, at which point the Germans switched the emphasis to political issues. At the end of July, Hitler and Ribbentrop put together outline proposals for an agreement with Russia based on the partition of Poland and the Baltic states. As the projected date for the invasion of Poland drew nearer, Hitler grew increasingly anxious to conclude a deal with Stalin. On 19 August, an economic agreement was signed and four days later Ribbentrop was received in Moscow and a non-aggression pact between Germany and Soviet Russia was signed.

The pact stipulated that, if either party became involved in war, the other would give no help to the enemy, nor would either of the powers join any group directed against the other. The agreement was to come into effect immediately it was signed by both parties. The price for Stalin's support was contained in a secret protocol which provided that, if territorial changes were to take place in Poland, the country was to be partitioned, with Germany taking the western area and Russia the Byelorussian and Ukrainian provinces, as well as Lublin and part of Warsaw. Russia was also to be allowed a free hand in Finland, Estonia and Latvia while Germany was assigned a free hand in Lithuania. Germany also agreed to recognize Russia's interest in the Romanian province of Bessarabia. In the light of such expansive territorial bargaining, it was, perhaps, hardly surprising that Stalin had found the German terms for an agreement infinitely more appealing in the short term than those of Britain and France. While the respite for Soviet Russia might be short, it none the less gave Stalin time to consolidate a large sphere of influence in eastern Europe and to build up Soviet military strength.

The conclusion of the Nazi–Soviet pact completely isolated Poland and laid it open to attack, without any immediate prospect of British or French military assistance. Hitler pressed ahead with plans for an invasion, telling senior commanders on 22 August that the aim of the war was the wholesale, and rapid, destruction of Poland, and that this time he was not going to be deprived of a war through last-minute negotiations. Yet there were still two unwelcome developments which took place in the last week of August, and which caused Hitler to pause momentarily. Firstly, on 25 August, Britain and Poland signed a Treaty of Alliance and the

British and French governments made it clear that, despite the Nazi–Soviet pact, they would stand by their promises of military assistance by whatever means to Poland. Then Mussolini, responding to an urgent German letter announcing that a strike against Poland was imminent, shocked Hitler by telling him that Italy was in no position to offer military assistance at the present time. Hitler hesitated – but only for a day. German troops invaded Poland on 1 September, and on 3 September Britain and France declared war on Germany. Twenty years after the end of the First World War, Europe found itself engulfed in another major conflict.

From European war to world war: Europe and the Far East, 1939–41

The German invasion of Poland in itself did not bring into being a major European or world war. Polish resistance was quickly crushed, and the country was rapidly defeated by a combination of German armies invading from the west and Soviet troops joining in from the east. After just five weeks, the fighting was over. But neither Britain nor France would accept a peace based on the German conquest of Poland, which they now realized would be followed by further military aggression.

For his part, Hitler had already told his senior commanders that he intended to turn west and to smash France as soon as possible, and then to bring England to its knees. On 18 October, he signed the plans under Operation Yellow, which set out an attack on France through Luxembourg, Belgium and the Netherlands. Only bad winter weather held Hitler back until the spring, and then the real European onslaught began. In April 1940, German troops somewhat unexpectedly invaded Denmark and Norway, meeting with little resistance in Denmark. Fighting in Norway continued for two months, but meanwhile the anticipated German offensive in western Europe started on 10 May, and resulted in spectacular and rapid success. The Netherlands were invaded and defeated in less than a week, and Belgium held the Germans up only for a further three weeks. Six weeks later, France had been defeated, and the victorious German troops entered Paris on 14 June. The northern two-thirds of France were occupied, and the remaining one-third, its capital now at Vichy, signed an armistice with Germany, and with Italy, which had entered the war four days before the Germans reached Paris. Hitler had conquered a large part of mainland Europe, and his allies occupied much of the rest. Only Britain for the time being lay beyond his grasp.

While Hitler now hesitated about whether or not to launch an invasion of Britain, Germany's hold over continental Europe was consolidated both economically and politically. By the end of 1940, Greater Germany included Austria, the Sudetenland, much of Poland, Alsace-Lorraine, Luxembourg and two former provinces of Belgium, Eupen and Malmedy. German Governors General ruled in Bohemia and Moravia and in part of Poland, and Slovakia had become a protectorate under German control. Denmark, Norway, Holland, Belgium and much of France were occupied by the German army. Germany dictated the terms of trade, specifying which countries should supply agricultural produce, raw materials or fuel in return for German industrial goods. Even unoccupied Sweden and Finland were drawn into Germany's economic system, because of their prized raw materials, in particular Swedish iron ore. Occupied countries were also expected to provide labour at cheap rates, or sometimes for no pay at all.

If the impact of German victory in west and central Europe in this first stage of the war was primarily economic and political, in the east, starting in Poland, it was aggressively racial. Most Poles in the German-occupied part were stripped of their citizenship, turned out of secondary schools and universities, and forced to work in menial jobs for their German masters. Germans were not to mix with or cohabit with Poles. All Polish leaders and members of the intelligentsia were to be killed, and Jews were to be rounded up and confined to increasingly overcrowded ghettos where they were starved and fell easy victims to contagious diseases. From 1941, mass killings of Jewish communities began to take place.

While Hitler was consolidating Germany's hold over Europe in 1940 and 1941, in the Far East Japan was successfully engaged in imposing a 'new order' on China and on south-east Asia. In 1937, Japanese troops had been drawn into a full-scale invasion of China, partly to eliminate Chinese communism, partly to secure important strategic materials and economic resources, and partly to bring the Chinese people into an 'Asian alliance' which was aimed at removing western imperialism and economic interests from the Pacific region. By the end of 1938, Japan controlled much of the Chinese mainland, though the government of Chiang Kai-Shek had retreated inland to a base in Szechwan province, and strong pockets of Chinese communist guerrillas continued to harry Japanese troops in northern and central China. In the course of 1938, Japanese troops based in Manchuria were also drawn into two major frontier clashes with Soviet Russia, which resulted in extensive fighting. Soviet troops emerged victorious from both, which increased the desire of the Japanese government to turn the anti-comintern pact, which they had signed with Germany in 1936, into a stronger alliance. Accordingly, in September 1940, Japan concluded the tripartite pact with Germany and Italy which bound the three powers to 'assist one another with all political, economic and military means' if any one of them was attacked by a country 'not involved in the current struggles'. And, in a further move to stabilize the Manchurian–Inner Mongolian frontier and to neutralize the threat of a Russian attack, in April 1941 Japan concluded a non-aggression pact with Soviet Russia.

This left Japan free to concentrate its expanding military and naval forces to the south of China and to work to create a 'single sphere' for the peoples of east and south-east Asia, in which Japanese ascendancy as the 'stabilizing force' could secure their 'common well-being and prosperity'. Clearly, this would necessitate the invasion and occupation of French and British colonial possessions in the area, and provoke war with Britain, for which Japan needed to be prepared. But the ultimate objectives of expansion for the Japanese leaders were both racial and economic: to create a Greater East Asia Co-Prosperity Sphere, along the lines of the New Order in east Asia, which would include the Netherlands East Indies, French Indo-China, Thailand, Malaya, Burma and the Philippines. In this sphere, Asian (but largely Japanese) leadership would prevail, and the peoples of the region (but, again, mainly of Japan) would enjoy access to the important raw materials and markets it contained. In the course of 1940, as the German armies overran much of Europe, the vision of the Japanese government expanded considerably. Japan's 'living sphere' was now defined as encompassing French Indo-China, Thailand, Malaya, Borneo, the Netherlands East Indies, Burma, India, Australia and New Zealand. Clearly, the achievement of such a 'sphere' would involve the destruction of the British, French and Dutch colonies in the region. For a campaign on that scale, Japan desperately needed a continuing supply of iron and steel, scrap metal and, above all else, oil, resources of which the islands

61

of Japan themselves were crucially short. While some of these vital minerals were available in northern China, or could be negotiated with the Netherlands East Indies regime, the largest supplier was the United States, which continued to supply around half of Japan's oil imports and large quantities of scrap iron until the summer of 1940.

It was at this point that the conflicts in Europe and in Asia began to come together in a more concerted way, when it became clear to the United States government that the parlous position of Britain at Germany's mercy in Europe and the Japanese threat to the British empire in Asia were combining to present a serious threat to the United States' own security. The fall of France might open the way to the extension of German influence over the French colonies in the Caribbean. If Britain was defeated, or sued for peace, German power might extend over the Atlantic Ocean. And in the Far East, in September 1940, the American ambassador in Tokyo reported to Washington that 'American interests in the Pacific are definitely threatened by [Japan's] policy of southward expansion, which is a thrust at the British Empire in the East'. Because the existence of the British empire was itself an element in America's security system, 'we must strive by every means to preserve the status quo in the Pacific, at least until the war in Europe has been won or lost'. As German power extended across Europe, and encouraged Japan to bring forward the plans for its own military advance southwards, the United States began to place restrictions on scrap metal and oil exports to Japan, and followed this up with the embargo of supplies of iron and steel. In 1941, brass, copper and zinc were added, thus forcing Japan to consider more precipitate military action in south Asia to seize vital oil and mineral supplies. Military invasion of French Indo-China in July 1941 was met by the United States with a freeze on Japanese assets in America and a complete embargo on oil exports. Japan could not fight a sustained military campaign without oil and steel, and thus army and navy leaders resolved that a military campaign would have to be launched in December 1941 at the latest in a desperate bid to replenish its stockpiles of the crucial resources.

In an audacious opening strike on 7 December, 1941, planes from the Japanese fleet attacked the main American Pacific naval base at Pearl Harbor in Hawaii, to ensure that the American fleet would be in no position to prevent Japanese military expansion in south Asia.

In the short term, the Japanese, like the Germans, were hugely successful. By the end of April 1942, the Japanese army had occupied Hong Kong, the Philippines, the Malayan peninsula, Burma, the Netherlands East Indies and most of the islands of the central and south-western Pacific. Thailand and French Indo-China were under Japanese domination, and the Greater East-Asia Co-Prosperity Sphere was brought into being. But the price was high. As a result of the attack on Pearl Harbor, the United States entered the war, and the newly established Japanese Pacific empire was to come under sustained attack from sea and from air for the next three years, until finally Japan itself was brought to its knees in 1945 by the dropping of two atom bombs.

In the months before the United States formally declared war on Japan, it was playing an increasingly important role in assisting Britain to continue the struggle against Germany and Italy. The Lend-Lease Act enabled Britain to continue to receive vital supplies from the United States. The United States navy was assisting Britain in the unfolding battle for supremacy in the Atlantic and was targeting German submarines for attack. Growing United States intervention enraged Hitler, and thus he received news of the Japanese attack on Pearl Harbor with great delight.

His instant reaction was that 'We can't lose the war at all . . . We now have an ally which has never been conquered in 3,000 years'. And Goebbels wrote in his diary on 9 December that 'Through the outbreak of war between Japan and the USA, a complete shift in the general world picture has taken place. The United States will scarcely now be in a position to transport worthwhile material to England, let alone the Soviet Union.' Elated by the turn of events in the Pacific, Hitler now declared war on the United States on 11 December 1941. The two conflicts, in Europe and in the Far East, had finally come together in a worldwide struggle for supremacy.

Earlier in 1941, Hitler had decided to abandon attempts to invade Britain, or to bomb it into submission, and to turn instead to a full-scale invasion of Soviet Russia, a confrontation which Hitler had long envisaged as both inevitable and crucial both in the continuing racial struggle against world Jewry and for the establishment of total German mastery in Europe. In June 1941, over 3 million German troops invaded in three distinct army groups and in the first few weeks made rapid progress. But they began to meet with serious Russian military resistance and, by the end of the year, the freezing

Russian winter had brought the German advance to a halt. The epic and brutal struggles which ensued in the following two years between the German and Russian forces in themselves transformed the scale of the war, as well as bringing into being an allied coalition of Soviet Russia, the United States and Britain united in waging a war of survival, and ultimately of counter-attack, against the Axis powers of Germany, Italy and Japan. Thus Germany's initial invasion of Poland, its subsequent failure to take Britain out of the war, and its alliances with Italy and, more importantly, with Japan, had finally brought about a major world war.

3

The historical debate

The historical debate about the origins of the Second World War began in earnest as the last shots were fired and the few remaining emaciated and pitiful concentration camp victims were freed by allied soldiers. Allied forces in Germany had captured large quantities of official German documents, and extracts from them now furnished the main evidence for the Nuremberg trials which were held between November 1945 and October 1946. The main charge against the twenty-two Nazi and German leaders brought before the war crimes tribunal, which set the tone for a decade or so of writing on the origins of the war, is worth setting out at length:

The aims and purposes of the Nazi Party . . . were . . . to accomplish the following by any means deemed opportune, including unlawful means, and contemplating ultimate resort to threat of force, force and aggressive war: i) to abrogate and overthrow the Treaty of Versailles and its restrictions upon the military armaments and activity of Germany; ii) to acquire the territories lost by Germany as the result of the World War of 1914–18 and other territories in Europe asserted by the Nazi conspirators to be occupied principally by so-called 'racial Germans'; iii) to acquire still further territories in continental Europe and elsewhere claimed by the Nazi conspirators to be required by the 'racial Germans' as 'Lebensraum' or living space, all at the expense of neighbouring and other countries. The aims and purposes of the Nazi conspirators were not fixed or static but evolved and expanded as they acquired progressively greater power and became able to make more effective application of threats of force and threats of aggressive war. When their expanding aims and purposes became finally so great as to provoke such strength of resistance as could be overthrown only by armed force and aggressive war, . . . the Nazi conspirators deliberately planned, determined upon, and launched their aggressive wars and wars in violation of international treaties, agreements and assurances . . .

Hitler and fellow Nazi leaders were not only guilty of causing the war. They had also, according to the Nuremberg Military Tribunal, committed 'crimes against Humanity in the course of preparation for war and in the course of prosecution of war', and were guilty of a conspiracy to 'commit War Crimes not only against the armed forces of their enemies but also against non-belligerent civilian populations'. At the end of the hearings, twelve defendants were sentenced to death, three to life imprisonment, a further four to long-term imprisonment, and three were acquitted. Hitler himself, of course, escaped the indignity of an appearance before the Tribunal, having committed suicide in his Berlin bunker right at the end of the war.

At the same time, the victorious wartime allies established a War Crimes Tribunal in Tokyo, which investigated the charge that Japan's leaders from 1931 had conspired to wage an aggressive, premeditated and imperialist war in Asia and against the western powers. At the end of the hearings, the Tribunal upheld the charge, and, as a result, sentenced twenty-five Japanese leaders, seven to death and the remainder to life imprisonment. Other war crimes trials were held in Hong Kong, Singapore and Borneo, and over 900 Japanese detainees were executed, having been found guilty of cruelty and of committing war crimes against local people and prisoners of war.

In the decade or so after the war, historians accepted these verdicts. Elisabeth Wiskemann, in *The Rome–Berlin Axis* (1949) wrote of 'Hitler's fundamental intention to dominate the world in order to establish his caste system which could not be achieved without war'. In *The Last Days of Hitler* (first published in 1947), Hugh Trevor-Roper argued that 'the conquest of Russia, the extermination of the Slavs, and the colonization of the East' were the 'real message of Nazism' and 'the burden of *Mein Kampf*'. While Hitler waged a traditional war in the West, of 'diplomatic aims and limited objectives in which some residue of international convention was regarded', the war in the East was a 'crusade, a "war of ideologies", in which all conventions were ignored'. Alan Bullock, in his classic biography, *Hitler, a Study in Tyranny* (1952), had a chapter entitled 'Hitler's War, 1939'. All three historians drew attention to Hitler's megalomania, his lust for domination and for destruction, and his growing madness. And for an older historian, meditating on the origins of the war already in 1940, the issue seemed even more clear-cut. G.P. Gooch, who had spent a distinguished historical career researching the origins of the First World War, wrote in the *Contemporary Review* in July 1940 that

> While the responsibilities of the war of 1914 remain a subject of controversy, the conflict which began with the German attack on Poland on September 1st, 1939, presents few difficulties to the historian. Opinions naturally differ on the use of their victory by the Allies during the 'twenties and on Anglo-French policy in regard to the dissatisfied Powers since 1931; but the revelation of Hitler's Napoleonic ambitions in March 1939, quickly followed by demands incompatible with Polish independence, places the guilt of the new conflagration squarely on his shoulders.

However, the rapid breakdown of relations between the United States and Soviet Russia at the end of the war, and the onset of the Cold War, set the scene for the emergence of somewhat different interpretations of the conflict. In January 1948 the American State Department published a collection of documents drawn from the captured German archives and entitled *Nazi–Soviet Relations*. In emphasizing the pre-war cooperation between the two countries, and especially the conclusion of the infamous Pact in August, 1939, the publication cast some of the blame for the outbreak of war in 1939 on Stalin. And in the same year, the Soviet Information Bureau published a volume entitled *The Falsifiers of History*, blaming American bankers and industrialists for providing the capital for the growth of German war industries in the 1920s and 1930s, and accusing Britain and France of deliberating encouraging Hitler to expand to the east. As the Soviet Union strengthened its grip on eastern Europe in the late 1940s, and as the Iron Curtain descended, such Marxist critiques emphasizing the role of big business and of capitalists, in Germany and elsewhere, in aiding and abetting Hitler's expansionist ambitions, and stressing the importance of the crisis of capitalism in bringing fascist regimes to power, became increasingly common in official East German and Polish publications, as well as in Soviet accounts of the origins of the war.

In Britain, however, in the years immediately after the war, the focus for debate was not on Hitler's ambitions, which seemed fairly clear-cut, or on those who helped him to realize them, but on the 'guilty men', those western leaders who failed to grasp his evil intentions early enough and who appeased him until it was too late. The distinguished historical authority on the politics of the reign of George III, Sir Lewis Namier, wrote a book in 1950 entitled *Diplomatic Prelude* in which he argued:

> The issue of a crisis depends not so much on its magnitude as on the courage and resolution with which it is met. The second German bid for world domination found Europe weak and divided. At several junctures it could have been stopped without excessive effort or sacrifice, but was not: a failure of European statesmanship . . . the rest of Europe had neither the faith, nor the will, nor even sufficient repugnance, to offer timely, effective resistance . . . Janissaries and appeasers aided Hitler's work: a failure of European morality.

This harsh verdict on the British and French leaders of the 1930s was echoed by Winston Churchill, who subtitled his book *The Gathering Storm* (volume I of his account of *The Second World War*), 'How the English-speaking peoples through their unwisdom, carelessness and good nature allowed the wicked to rearm'. According to Churchill, the war should have been called 'The Unnecessary War' since 'There never was a war more easy to stop'. However, Namier, Churchill and others who had wanted Britain to take a stand against German aggression much earlier than in 1939 did not always agree on the exact point at which resistance to Hitler would have been most effective. Churchill believed that the allies should have intervened in 1934 or 1935 to prevent Nazi Germany from rearming, and particularly from establishing a powerful air force. Others felt that Britain and France should have taken a strong stand over the remilitarization of the Rhineland, and that the threat of force, or actual military intervention, would have deterred Hitler from further expansion. Many people still felt the shame of the Munich 'sell-out' and the betrayal of Czechoslovakia, and attacked British and French leaders for agreeing in October 1938 to the incorporation of the Sudetenland into Germany, thus paving the way for the dismemberment of the Czech republic some five months later.

Throughout the 1950s and early 1960s, the 'appeasers', as Chamberlain, Hoare, Lord Halifax, Laval and Bonnet were disparagingly called, received a universally hostile press. They were portrayed as stupid and pathetic men, frightened to stand up to Hitler and prepared instead to offer up territories and peoples in eastern Europe in a vain attempt to satisfy Hitler's insatiable appetite. It was argued that they should have realized by 1936 at the latest that they were dealing with a tyrant who needed to be stopped at the earliest opportunity. But instead, they continued to seek an accommodation with the Nazi regime, despite the escalating price exacted by Hitler. *The Appeasers*, written by two Oxford graduates in their mid-twenties, Martin Gilbert and Richard Gott and published in 1963, was the first comprehensive treatment of the factors shaping inter-war British appeasement, but its verdict on Chamberlain was nevertheless still a harsh one. In their view, 'British policy, far from appeasing Hitler, showed him that the British Government were willing to come to terms with him at the expense of other nations'. Appeasement was 'an attempt to move closer to Germany, despite German domestic brutality and eastward expansion. It failed.'

In this immediate post-war period, German historians were concerned not so much with Hitler's expansionist aims and British and French failure to check them as with his rise to power and the extent to which he was supported by the German electorate. They drew attention to the shabby political intrigues which brought him the Chancellorship, and to the fact that over 50 per cent of the German electorate had failed to support the Nazis in the election of 1933 despite the widespread intimidation. Detailed studies began to show that Hitler's Germany was not an efficient and effective dictatorship but a ramshackle structure, with competing spheres of influence containing uneasy compromises between the old ruling elites and the new Nazi rulers. There was resistance to Hitler's rule, though it was sporadic and often concealed from public view.

But the debate about the role of Hitler in relation to the outbreak of the Second World War, and the extent to which he was aided and abetted by British and French appeasement policies, really took off in earnest with the publication in 1961 of A.J.P. Taylor's *Origins of the Second World War*, a book which was to exert an enormous influence over students and general readers alike in the course of the following forty years. Alan Taylor was a well-respected historian of modern German and European history, about which he had written widely and eloquently, in works such as *The Course of German History* and *The Habsburg Monarchy*. He now sought to examine Hitler and the foreign policy of Nazi Germany in the context of recent German and European diplomatic history. While he followed previous historians in criticizing western leaders for their inconsistent policies, he added two additional ingredients, the first of which quickly raised the temperature of the historical debate to boiling point. For he asserted that Hitler, far from being a uniquely villainous German leader, was merely continuing the policy of previous German governments in seeking eastward expansion. The basic problem confronting European statesmen after 1919, argued Taylor, was not Hitler or the expansionist ideology of National Socialism, but German ambitions which had been checked but not completely crushed by the First World War.

Taylor claimed that, in aiming to make Germany the 'dominant power in Europe and maybe, more remotely in the world', Hitler was pursing ambitions no different from those held by German leaders before 1914 or by Stresemann and other Weimar leaders in the 1920s. 'He was in part the creation of Versailles, in part the creation of ideas that were common in contemporary Europe. Most of all, he was the creation of German history and of the German present', Taylor asserted, and furthermore reminded readers that 'He would have counted for nothing without the support and co-operation of the German people . . . In principle and in doctrine Hitler was no more wicked and unscrupulous than many other contemporary statesmen.' However Taylor did concede that 'in wicked acts he outdid them all'. Interestingly, the publication in the same year of the first of Professor Fritz Fischer's meticulously researched volumes on imperial German foreign policy up to and into the First World War, *Griff nach der Weltmacht*, which was not translated into English until 1966, exposed for the first time the scale of German annexationist ambitions in central and eastern Europe in the early part of the century, thus giving considerable credibility to Taylor's 'continuity' thesis. This was a point which Taylor seized upon in the foreword to the 1964 Penguin reprint of his book, when he added fuel to the flames by asserting that Hitler, far from transcending German First World War leaders such as Bethmann-Hollweg and Ludendorff in his ambitions, 'was actually being more moderate than they when he sought only *Lebensraum* in the east and repudiated, in *Mein Kampf*, gains in the west'.

Thus the vital question for Taylor centred not on Hitler's policies but on those of the western leaders. Given aggressive German ambitions and an unresolved 'German problem' in the period after 1919, why did British and French leaders not resist German claims in the mid-1930s, and then why did they suddenly, in 1939, decide to take a stand over Poland? Taylor's book therefore shifted the debate away from Hitler, the planner and architect of war, to Hitler the opportunist, whose traditional if substantial German appetite was continually being whetted by the concessions offered to him by British and French leaders whenever he raised the question of German grievances. Hitler himself, according to Taylor, had no concrete plans. There was 'no clear dividing line in his mind between political ingenuity and small wars, such as the attack on Poland. The one thing he did not plan was the great war often attributed to him.' In fact, Taylor alleged, extremely controversially, that 'Hitler hoped to get by without war at all'. Instead, he merely seized opportunities as they arose. The Austrian crisis of March 1938 'was produced by Schuschnigg not by Hitler'. The Sudeten crisis was created by the Sudeten Nazis who 'built up the tension gradually, without guidance from Hitler'; Hitler then 'merely took advantage of it'. After October 1938, Hitler knew that the Munich settlement could not work, since an 'independent Czechoslovakia could not survive when deprived of her natural frontiers and with Czech prestige broken'. The result, 'neither sinister nor premeditated', was a German occupation of Prague, followed by a Polish crisis forced on him by the Polish Foreign Minister Beck. Hitler was not really planning for war in 1939, and the proof of this, according to Taylor, lay in the level of German rearmament by 1939, which was by no means great enough to sustain a European, let alone a world, war. Indeed, in a final flourish which is remembered by generations of students, Taylor concluded that Hitler 'became involved in war through launching on 29 August a diplomatic manoeuvre which he ought to have launched on 28 August. Such were the origins of the second World war . . .'

Not surprisingly, Taylor's interpretation, brilliantly written and persuasively argued, caused howls of protest and unleashed a torrent of replies and rebuttals. But as Professor Max Beloff commented perceptively at the time, in the *Sunday Telegraph*, 'no one who has digested this enthralling work will ever be able to look at the period again in quite the same way'. Those historians who were appalled by Taylor's cavalier use of primary evidence and by the conclusions he reached produced detailed rebuttals and scholarly articles taking issue with his general thesis and drawing attention to his selective use and abuse of source material. There were arguments over the significance, or otherwise, of the Hossbach memorandum of 1937, over the extent to which *Mein Kampf* could be viewed as a 'blueprint' for subsequent aggression by Hitler, and about the importance or otherwise of Hitler's unpublished *Second Book* of 1928, his *Table Talk* and his speeches to army and business leaders and at rallies. The effect of the growing controversy was to widen considerably the scope of the debate about the origins of the Second World War, and to stimulate research into a number of important fields such as Nazi ideology, continuity and change in inter-war German foreign policy, the factors shaping Nazi foreign policy after 1933, and the extent to which Hitler and the Nazis were preparing Germany for war by 1938. Though Taylor's account remained enormously popular and accessible to students and to general readers, its narrow focus on diplomacy and its narrative approach to Anglo-German relations within an exclusively European context was looking distinctly outdated and inadequate a decade or two later in light of the extensive research which was undertaken in the 1960s and 1970s, not just into Nazi foreign policy and the responses to it in Europe, but into Soviet, Japanese and United States ambitions as well.

One of the major criticisms levelled at Taylor's account was that it omitted any mention of the fundamental ideological beliefs which shaped Nazi foreign policy and gave it consistency. Gerhard Weinberg, a German-born academic working on captured German documents in the United States after the war, discovered and published Hitler's *Second Book*, which had been written in 1928 but not published during Hitler's lifetime. On the evidence of this and of the extensive documentation he studied, Weinberg argued, in a

72

book published in 1970 entitled *The Foreign Policy of Hitler's Germany: Diplomatic Revolution in Europe 1933–36*, that, far from being a pure opportunist, Hitler in fact 'had some very definite, fixed ideas on foreign policy before he came to power' and that 'during the years from 1933 to 1939 Hitler kept these ideas very much in mind in the actual conduct of affairs, though he tended to reserve oral and written expression of them to the privacy of the conference room or the circle of his associates'. According to Weinberg, 'Hitler's ideology consisted primarily of two related systems of ideas', revolving around 'race' and 'space'. German recovery could be based only on its natural racial superiority, which would require social and health policies geared to producing a racially pure population and the elimination both of those of racially weak stock and, more urgently, of those in Germany of alien race such as the Jews. A racially strong and expanding German population would require more space, defined by Hitler as agriculturally useful land. Thus an 'adjustment of space to population' would have to take place, through

> the conquest of additional land areas whose native population would be expelled or exterminated, not assimilated. The availability of such land areas would in turn encourage the good, healthy Nordic couples settled on them to raise large families that would both make up for the casualties incurred in the conquest of the territory and assure adequate military manpower for subsequent wars *they* would need to wage.

Thus, space would be secured through a relentless process of struggle which was potentially never-ending since, as Weinberg pointed out, 'if space is to be adjusted to an expanded population by conquest, and such conquest again enables the population to expand and facilitates further conquest, the only possible limitations are utter defeat on the one hand or total occupation of the globe on the other'. In an earlier article, published in 1964 in the *Journal of Modern History*, Weinberg had referred to a comment by Rudolf Hess, Hitler's companion in Landsberg prison, that Hitler was of the opinion that world peace could come only 'when one power, the racially best one, has attained complete and uncontested supremacy'. It would then establish a world police and assure itself 'the necessary living space . . . The lower races will have to restrict themselves accordingly'. Hitler himself outlined the expansion process in his *Second Book* as he envisaged it would develop: 'We consider our (anticipated) sacrifices, weigh the size of the possible success, and will go on the attack, regardless of whether it will come to a stop 10 or 1,000 kilometres beyond the present lines. For wherever our success may end, that will always be only the starting point of a new fight.'

A fellow American academic, Norman Rich, who had also worked extensively on captured German Foreign Ministry documents of the Nazi period, endorsed Weinberg's view of the supreme importance to Nazi foreign policy of Hitler's ideology. In his book *Hitler's War Aims*, published in 1973, he wrote that

> The assumption that the past and future of human civilization depended exclusively on the Aryans, that therefore they alone among the peoples of the earth deserved to live and prosper – this was the basis on which rested the entire superstructure of Hitler's ideological program, his concept of the role of party and state, his plans for the future of the German people. Race, far from being a mere propagandistic slogan, was the very rock on which the Nazi church was built. Hitler never appears to have had any doubts about the literal truth of his racial theories, nor did his more fanatic followers.

As for expansionist aims, Hitler believed that

> If one wanted land and soil on the European continent, the conquests of real value for the future could be achieved by and large only at Russia's expense . . . there had to be a final reckoning with France, but the defeat of France would be a hollow victory if German policy were restricted thereto. The elimination of the French threat would have and would retain significance only if it provided the rear cover for an enlargement of the German domain in Eastern Europe. National Socialism, therefore, consciously abandoned the foreign policy of the Second Reich. Germany was to cease its fruitless pursuit of a colonial policy and above all, its drive to the south and west. The Third Reich intended to resume the Germanic expansionist program where it had stopped six hundred years ago, and to press once again over the routes of the medieval crusading orders into the lands of the east.

74

Thus to Weinberg and to Rich, Hitler was no opportunist but a man of unshakeable ideological convictions, which lay at the heart of his foreign policy after 1933. They rejected entirely Taylor's attempts to depict him, in Weinberg's words, as 'an eighteenth century diplomat, striving for revision of the most recent treaty in the same way Maria Theresa attempted to recover Silesia for Austria from the Prussia of Frederick the Great'. This view of Hitler was shared by a German historian, Eberhard Jäckel, in a book published in 1984, *Hitler in History*. Far from merely taking advantage of opportunities presented to him by the miscalculations of other European leaders, Jackel argued that Hitler had a clear vision of the future of the Third Reich. 'Perhaps never in history did a ruler write down before he came to power what he was to do afterward as precisely as did Adolf Hitler. Hitler set himself two goals: a war of conquest and the elimination of the Jews.' According to Jäckel,

> Hitler's ultimate goal was the establishment of a greater Germany than had ever existed before in history. The way to this greater Germany was a war of conquest fought mainly at the expense of Soviet Russia. It was in the east of the European continent that the German nation was to gain living space (*Lebensraum*) for generations to come. This expansion would in turn provide the foundation for Germany's renewed position as a world power. Militarily the war would be easy because Germany would be opposed only by a disorganised country of Jewish Bolsheviks and incompetent Slavs.

For all three historians, Hitler's ideology based on race, space and unceasing struggle decisively differentiated Nazi foreign policy from that of previous German regimes. They therefore completely rejected Taylor's argument that Hitler was merely pursuing traditional German foreign-policy goals, pointing out that Hitler himself had drawn a stark contrast between the objectives of previous German regimes and his own vision of the future. Whilst they acknowledged that German First World War leaders were aiming at the establishment of a *Mitteleuropa* or sphere of German domination in central and eastern Europe, this was in no way based on doctrines of race, and was part of a finite set of aims which was to be achieved within a generally accepted European diplomatic framework. Stresemann's foreign policy in the 1920s, whilst it sought to recover territories lost by Germany in 1919, was again conducted within a conventional diplomatic framework which sought to re-establish a strong Germany in the centre of Europe. Stresemann may well have envisaged future German hegemony over the newly created central European states of Poland, Czechoslovakia and Hungary, and even union with Austria, but he pursued his objectives through diplomatic means, and was certainly not planning wars of racial conquest. Unquestionably, there were common features shared by Weimar and Nazi foreign policy: a desire to overturn the Treaty of Versailles, to rearm, to reverse the verdict of the First World War and re-establish Germany once again as Europe's dominant power. But in no sense did Weinberg or Rich see Hitler as a typical German leader, aiming at the same goals as former German Chancellors or contemporary German leaders.

Hitler was not born a German subject and he could not be described as a typical German leader in terms of his background and education, or Hindenburg would not have referred to him so disparagingly as the 'Bohemian corporal'. He was born a German-speaking Habsburg subject, an *Ausländer*, one of hundreds of thousands in that part of Europe who looked to Germany as their homeland but were not German subjects. He rose to become German Chancellor despite lacking social connections, wealth or further education. In this respect he was more like Ebert, the first Social Democratic Chancellor in the Weimar government, but unlike Ebert he shared the expansionist ambitions of the German nationalists. There is no doubt at all that many of his aims, if not always his methods of achieving them, were supported by large numbers of Germans. Yet by 1938, army leaders and conservative nationalists were prepared to work against him. They were worried about his seemingly unlimited vision of German expansion, about his obsessive drive to realize it and about his ruthless determination to crush by one means or another all obstacles which stood in his way. They did not believe he was talking for effect, and some lost their jobs, and later their lives, as a result of their opposition to his plans. The aims and ambitions of traditional and typical German statesmen in peacetime were limited; many within Germany before 1939 opposed Hitler's policies because they seemed to have no limits. As the American historian Sally Marks has noted, Hitler's aims were more vast, his ideology very different and his methods much more confrontational than those of any previous German leaders. By the 1990s,

Taylor's interpretation of Hitler and of the origins of the Second World War had been vigorously rejected by the great majority of historians researching inter-war history. David Kaiser's verdict, in *Modern Germany Reconsidered*, edited by Gordon Martel and published in 1992, was that Taylor's views that 'Hitler did not intend war in 1939 and lacked a real plan for the conquest of Europe and of the world, and that other governments played a crucial role in unleashing German expansionism' can no longer be regarded as valid.

However, by this time, a new debate had been raging for some years about the extent to which the course of Nazi foreign policy had been decisively and exclusively shaped by Hitler. Norman Rich's view was straightforward and uncompromising, in asserting that 'one of the most remarkable features of the history of Germany under National Socialism was the extent to which Hitler imposed his personal authority on the German people and state. The point cannot be stressed too strongly. Hitler was master in the Third Reich'. This view was shared by Weinberg, by Jäckel, by Bullock and by the German historians Hildebrand and Hillgrüber. They were all in agreement that Hitler was driven by a number of ideological obsessions, that he followed a 'programme' if not a 'blueprint for action', to which he consistently adhered, from the mid-1920s until his death in his Berlin bunker, which was based on his ideological beliefs, and that he was in control of the policies implemented in the Third Reich, both domestic and foreign. The historians who held this view were labelled as 'programmatists' or 'intentionalists', and their views came under challenge in the 1970s and 1980s from a group of historians arguing that this was far too simplistic a view to take, and that the environment in which Hitler operated after 1933, the chaotic structure of the Third Reich, the many competing centres of power and the haphazard way in which decisions were taken were all major factors shaping Nazi domestic and foreign policies. Those who emphasized the importance of structural issues, of competing power blocs and of a variety of constraints on Hitler's power after 1933 were referred to as 'structuralists' or 'functionalists', and fierce argument and debate between the two schools of thought took place from the mid-1960s through to the 1990s.

Far from Hitler being master in the Third Reich, the German historian Hans Mommsen described him in 1971 as 'unwilling to take decisions, frequently uncertain, exclusively concerned with upholding his prestige and personal authority, influenced in the strongest fashion by his current entourage, in some respects a weak dictator'. In a chapter in Walter Laqueur's *Fascism: A Reader's Guide*, first published in 1976, Mommsen argued that 'the regime's foreign policy ambitions were many and varied, without clear aims, and only linked by the ultimate goal: hindsight alone gives them some air of consistency'. Instead, the Third Reich was marked by factional strife, by chaotic decision-making and by 'uncontrollable and uninhibited power conflicts between independent factions' which established 'a type of cumulative radicalization', which progressively destabilized the 'alliance of interests between the conservative elites and the fascist party' on which the Third Reich was based. In this interpretation, policies were driven not solely by Hitler as the 'fanatical instigator' but by army and business leaders, and by colleagues who seized upon Hitler's 'spur of the moment bright idea' and 'propaganda utterances . . . as orders for action' to demonstrate their 'diligence, the efficiency of their machinery and their political indispensability'. Thus, in Mommsen's view, the chaotic structure of the Third Reich and the incessant competition between individuals and factions for power and for Hitler's favour, rather than the ideology first expressed in *Mein Kampf*, crucially shaped Nazi foreign policy.

Another German historian, Martin Broszat, advanced a similar view in 1970, arguing that there was little evidence of a design or plan behind Hitler's foreign policy. Instead, the pursuit of *Lebensraum* in the east reflected Hitler's need to sustain, as Kershaw summarized it, 'the dynamic momentum he had helped unleash. In foreign policy this meant above all breaking all shackles of restraint, formal bonds, pacts or alliances, and the attainment of complete freedom of action, unrestricted by international law or treaty, in German power-political considerations'. For Broszat, 'the aim of winning *Lebensraum* in the east had until 1939 largely the function of an ideological metaphor, a symbol to account for ever new foreign policy activity'. For Broszat, as for Mommsen, it was the antagonistic forces at the heart of the Third Reich and the social dynamic of the Nazi movement which necessitated ceaseless action and drove Hitler and the regime inexorably towards turning the *Lebensraum* metaphor into reality. Again, in this interpretation, the structural and political context within which Hitler chose to operate after 1933, and the strong domestic pressures and tensions which it generated, were decisive in shaping Nazi foreign policy and in ensuring its constant radicalization.

One example of such tensions was the serious economic crisis which Germany faced after 1936, as a result of the adoption of the Four Year Plan and of ever more frenetic rearmament. The economic historian Tim Mason drew attention to a serious constraint on Hitler, arising from the lessons he drew from the German Revolution of 1918 of the dangers of mass working-class unrest. Hitler was acutely conscious of the need to placate the German working class after 1933, by making available cheap consumer goods and by keeping down food prices. This forced the regime to provide both 'Guns' and 'Butter' for the German popu-lation, placing great strain on the economy, which was further compounded by a growing labour shortage which enabled skilled workers to exploit their bargaining position. Thus Mason argued that the domestic political situation was responsible for a major economic crisis by the late 1930s, which also affected foreign trade, public finance and agriculture. He believed that the leaders of the Third Reich were well aware that they were confronting a critical domestic situation, and that this decisively influenced the course of the foreign policy they adopted. Thus conquest and war 'was an alternative to highly unpopular domestic measures' which the regime was reluctant to take, shown by its 'refusal to raise food prices and income tax rates, its refusal to ration petrol and its failure to make full use after June 1938 of powers to conscript male workers and to cut earnings'. In order to maintain social peace at home and to protect its own position, Mason argued that the Third Reich had to wage war sooner rather than later, and had to launch a series of 'smash and grab' raids on neighbouring countries to acquire the raw materials and economic resources it desperately needed to maintain and expand its armed strength without unduly exploiting its own domestic labour force. In an article in *Past and Present*, in December 1964, he concluded that 'a war for the plunder of manpower and materials lay square in the dreadful logic of German economic devel-opment under National Socialist rule'.

However, Mason's interpretation of a domestic crisis driving Nazi Germany to war in 1939 was strongly disputed by a fellow British economic historian, Richard Overy. Overy did not accept Mason's view that the German economy was 'out of control' by 1939 and that the regime was facing one of the most acute crises of the 1930s. For Overy, the year of economic crisis for Germany was 1932, when there were 8 million unemployed, gross national product had plunged by 45 per cent from 1928, the volume of trade had shrunk to less than half of what it had been four years previously, there was a massive loss of business and creditor confidence, and increasing social and political conflict and violence led to the collapse of parliamentary rule. In contrast, he pointed out that 1938 and 1939 were years of high growth, rising investment, full employment and falling interest rates, with capital and labour markets being regulated by the state. Admittedly, state regulation did not go smoothly, was piecemeal and often uncoordinated, and resulted in fierce competition from different sectors for increasingly scarce resources. But for Overy, that did not amount to a massive economic crisis which could be resolved only by war. Rather it was the growing 'primacy of politics' which was placing demands on the economy and not economic weakness, which in itself was the primary factor prompting Hitler to launch a war. Indeed, as Overy points out,

> the chemical and explosives programme, the aluminium programme, Buna rubber [a form of synthetic rubber], synthetic fuel oil, domestic iron-ore output, the Westwall . . . were all well under way or completed by 1939. The state had successfully diverted 60% of industrial investment to the programmes of the Four Year Plan . . . Hitler's demands were not simple additions, but represented a gradual switch away from investment in the basic programme of economic rearmament to the output of manufactured weapons. The central problem faced by officials and managers was not the imminent collapse of the whole system, but its growing and manifest inefficiency . . .

Overy completely rejected the argument that the economic question as portrayed by Mason was 'the primary determinant in explaining the outbreak of general war in September 1939'. Instead, he cited a wealth of issues, political, military and strategic as well as economic, which influenced Hitler to prepare for war against Poland in the autumn of 1939. In particular, Overy drew attention to the conviction which Hitler had developed after the Munich crisis, that 'Britain and France would not fight seriously for Poland, or would not fight at all if Hitler called their bluff'. Hitler believed that 'the west had bankrupted its stock at Munich, and that the balance of power was moving in Germany's favour . . . in the aftermath of Munich and then Prague Hitler was determined to get his free hand in the east and not to be denied it again'. Overy agrees that 'War with Poland would solve some of the economic problems, would help to keep the regime on the boil, and would bring [Hitler] widespread popular support and give his soldiers a first taste of blood. In this sense the war had a domestic dimension as well, and was not just 'foreign policy'. But most of all he saw a window of opportunity opening up, and did not want to lose it.' Thus Overy takes us firmly back to the view of Hitler taking the important foreign policy decisions, albeit within the constraints imposed by the structure and political contours of the Third Reich.

This view was strongly endorsed by Gerhard Weinberg in 1980, in his comprehensive diplomatic history of pre-war Nazi Germany, when he concluded that

> The power of Germany was directed by Adolf Hitler. Careful analyses by scholars have revealed internal divisions, organisational confusions, jurisdictional battles, institutional rivalries, and local deviations behind the façade of monolithic unity that the Third Reich liked to present to its citizens and to the world in word and picture. The fact remains, however, that the broad lines of policy were determined in all cases by Hitler himself. Where others agreed, or at least did not object strenuously, they were allowed the choice of going along or retreating into silence, but on major issues of policy the Führer went his own way.

By the mid-1980s, in *The Nazi Dictatorship*, Ian Kershaw agreed with this assessment, when he concluded that 'There seems little disagreement among historians that Hitler did personally take the "big" decisions in foreign policy after 1933. Even the most forceful "structuralist" analyses accept that Hitler's "leadership monopoly" was far more in evidence in the foreign-policy decision-making process than in the realm of domestic policy'. David Kaiser supported this view in his chapter in *Modern Germany Reconsidered*, pointing out that Hitler was the prime mover who made the critical foreign-policy decisions – relating to rearmament in 1933, to the remilitarization of the Rhineland, and to *Anschluss* with Austria – 'often in the teeth of opposition from his diplomats and generals'. His successes only increased his authority over them.

By the 1990s, therefore, a consensus had emerged amongst historians that while 'there were forces at work, both within and outside

81

Germany, conditioning the framework of Hitler's actions', these 'structural determinants', as Kershaw noted, pushed Hitler 'if anything still faster on the path he was in any case determined to tread'. The major initiatives in German foreign policy in the 1930s can be traced to Hitler himself, and, while economic factors contributed to the framework within which decisions had to be made, they did not play a dominant role in Hitler's decisions. However, there still remained some areas of disagreement, relating to the exact nature of Hitler's 'plans' and about whether his ultimate aim was continental or world domination.

Forty years or so after the end of the Second World War, historians no longer regarded the work which Hitler had penned whilst in prison, *Mein Kampf*, as establishing a detailed blueprint for action, to be followed to the letter by Hitler, which would inevitably lead to war. Instead, there was now considerable agreement that Hitler had developed strongly obsessive and fixed ideas about foreign policy by the early 1920s, derived from his ideological beliefs, from which he did not subsequently deviate and which decisively shaped his foreign policy after 1933. Whilst these fixed ideas centred on the conquest of land in the east of Europe, necessitating sooner or later a war against Russia, and included the possibility of an alliance with England, Hitler had no clear idea in 1933 about how he would reach his goals. However, historians point out that he was very clear about his preliminary objectives, the urgent need for German rearmament and the removal of the shackles of the Treaty of Versailles, telling his army generals in 1933 about the importance of the 'struggle against Versailles' and the need to prepare for the conquest of new living space in the east. Once Germany's western flank had been safeguarded by the return of the Saar in 1935, the remilitarization of the Rhineland in 1936 and greatly increased levels of military strength, Hitler could then turn to pursue racial and territorial objectives in eastern Europe, bringing into Germany the German-speaking peoples of Austria, Czechoslovakia and Poland, and preparing for a struggle with Poland. But all the while, there was a bigger goal, making Germany ready for a major war against Russia, preceded, if necessary, by action against France and possibly Britain, if the latter refused an alliance with Germany.

There is some debate amongst historians about the extent to which these aims constituted a 'programme' which Hitler pursued in stages. The German historian Andreas Hillgrüber had suggested already in the 1960s that Hitler was following a *Stufenplan* or three-stage plan for establishing German hegemony first over Europe, then over the Middle East and other British colonial territory and, more distantly, over the United States and thus the whole world. Klaus Hildebrand agreed that Hitler pursued a 'carefully calculated stage by stage plan' which proceeded from the gaining of *Lebensraum* in eastern Europe to the destruction of the Soviet Union and ultimately aimed at an eventual 'war for world domination'. Other historians have rejected such a neat formulation, whilst not denying the driving forces and central aims of Hitler's foreign policy, but taking more note of Hitler's many improvisations, political opportunism and tactical flexibility. However, all agree that Hitler was preparing for a major conflict from the mid-1930s onwards, as evidenced by the adoption of the Four Year Plan in 1936, and the rapid build-up of Germany's war capacity. As Richard Overy's research has established, between 1936 and 1939 two-thirds of the German economy was devoted to preparing for war, with a quarter of the German work force, by 1939, directly engaged in war-related industries. In 1938, 52 per cent of government expenditure, and 17 per cent of Germany's gross domestic product was being spent on armaments, a level which exceeded the combined expenditure on armaments of Britain, France and the United States. In Overy's view, Hitler's prime objective was to prepare Germany for a major military confrontation with Russia, which he expected to take place at some point in the early 1940s; a war over Poland at an earlier date was not his main aim, though German armed forces were to be ready to fight, if necessary, to restore Danzig and the Polish corridor to Germany if the western powers were not willing to acquiesce in their return. Hence the reason why Nazi Germany was not fully geared up for European or world war in 1939 was not because the opportunist Hitler hoped to achieve his territorial goals without military conflict, as Taylor had argued in 1961, but rather because the Four Year Plan to make Germany ready for a major conflict in the east was not due to be fully completed until the early 1940s. At the same time, Overy has argued that, by the late 1930s, Hitler saw a window of opportunity opening up for Germany, in that he perceived Britain and France to be in inexorable decline, whilst the United States and Japan, two potential world powers, were not yet in a dominant position. Thus Nazi Germany needed to capitalize on this favourable situation, which was not likely to persist for very many years.

So, after the great showdown with Russia, was there to be a second conflict, to wrest control of the Middle East oil fields from the grip of the western democracies, and a third, against the United States, for global domination? Such evidence as we have is not conclusive, but those historians who believe that Hitler's ambitions did embrace eventual world domination point to the 'Z plan', adopted in January 1939, which was aimed at a huge expansion of Germany's navy. The plan gave priority to naval rearmament over other armed services, and envisaged the creation of a modern fleet by 1945 to include four pocket battleships by 1943, six larger battleships by 1944 and four aircraft carriers. The objective was clearly to enable Germany to be ready for conflict with the world's leading naval powers – the United States, Britain and possibly also Japan. Alongside this naval expansion, resources were also to be made available for the development of long-range bombers which would have the capability to fly to America and back, the 'America bomber' as the model came to be called. Further supporting evidence that Hitler was already looking ahead to a conflict against the United States for world domination comes in the form of information received by the United States Ambassador in Paris, William Bullitt, in the year before the outbreak of war, which he quickly passed on to President Roosevelt. According to Bullitt's source, Otto von Habsburg, Hitler had held a meeting at Berchtesgaden on 8 March 1939, at which he emphasized that German survival depended on seizing sources of raw materials and eliminating Germany's enemies, namely the Jews and the democracies. Thus Prague was to be occupied before Easter 1939, Poland, Hungary and Romania would be forced into the Nazi orbit by the end of the summer, and in the following year, with the extensive resources of the *Mitteleuropa* which had been established, Germany would crush France, the hereditary enemy, dominate Britain, and then launch 'the greatest operation in all history, an attack on the United States'. Hitler was quoted as saying that Germany would no longer have to suffer insults from President Roosevelt. 'We will settle accounts with the Jews of the dollar . . . we will exterminate the Jewish democracy, and Jewish blood will mix itself with the dollars'. However, this was fairly soon after the events of *Kristallnacht*, about which President Roosevelt had had the temerity to remonstrate with Hitler, thus perhaps provoking a characteristically explosive response from the German dictator. Nevertheless, the first part of Hitler's prophecy proved to be chillingly accurate.

Undoubtedly, if Nazi Germany had been victorious over Soviet Russia as a result of the launch of Operation Barbarossa (the Nazi code-name for the invasion) in 1941, and Hitler was consequently in a position to establish a Nazi stranglehold over the whole of the European continental landmass from France and the Low Countries across to the Urals, it is difficult to imagine that he would not have been planning further campaigns to extend Nazi influence. Global conflicts against the British empire and against the United States for world domination might well have followed. But this takes us into the realms of speculation, where the evidence is patchy and inconclusive. What we can say is that historians are now generally agreed that by 1939 Hitler was gearing Germany up for a major conflict, not over Poland which he expected to conquer without serious opposition from the western democracies, but with Bolshevik Russia. At the same time, his contempt for France and anger at Britain, for having refused to become a junior partner in the Aryan conquest of Europe, was giving rise to the possibility of an attack in the west before the great showdown with Russia, once the western democracies had made clear their opposition to the Nazi invasion of Prague in March 1939, and their intention to support Polish opposition to German demands for the return of Danzig and the Polish corridor.

Thus the debate has shifted in recent years to look afresh at British and French diplomacy in the inter-war period, and particularly after Munich, and to assess why an alliance between the western powers and Russia, with the aim of containing German aggression, was not concluded. In the past twenty-five years, British and French appeasement policies have been reappraised, in the light of newly available archival sources, and the contempt of an earlier generation of historians has been replaced by a much more sympathetic understanding of the strategic dilemmas facing British and French statesmen in the shadow of the Great War. Historians such as Paul Kennedy, in *The Realities Behind Diplomacy* and *The Rise and Fall of British Naval Mastery*, and David Reynolds, in *Britannia Overruled*, have drawn attention to the steady decline in British naval and economic power since the late nineteenth century in the face of aggressive challenges from Germany and from the United States, and the serious effect of the Great War on British trade and finances. Anthony Adamthwaite, in his study of inter-war French strategy and diplomacy, *Grandeur and Misery*, has similarly highlighted French military and economic weakness in the 1920s, a theme also taken up by many American historians, amongst them Stephen Shuker, William McDougall and Sally Marks. All these historians stress the extent to which the First World War had impoverished Britain and particularly France. With massive war debts to pay off, and markets to recapture, both countries sought stability in Europe and looked to the United States for economic and military assistance both in enforcing the peace settlement and in promoting European recovery. But instead the American government repudiated President Wilson's diplomacy, and withdrew from European involvement, leaving Britain and France to police the settlement alone, in the face of a new challenge, the emergence of Bolshevik Russia. This new ideologically driven regime, weakened but not crushed by the civil war which was fiercely contested until 1921, vowed to overthrow the capitalist government enemies which it claimed were encircling it, not by external aggression but by fomenting revolution within the capitalist states themselves. At the same time, Russian leaders singled out the British empire as a particular enemy, with Zinoviev in 1920 calling for a 'holy war . . . against British Imperialism'. British Foreign Secretary Curzon described the 'Russian menace in the East' in the early 1920s as 'incomparably greater than anything else that has happened in my lifetime to the British Empire'.

Thus fear of communism was a major factor shaping appeasement policies in the 1920s and 1930s, as ideological conflict and class warfare divided countries and spread across Europe. This was yet another factor driving the British and French governments to increase expenditure on economic and social recovery, in a bid to stave off worker militancy and alienation. But this meant that money was not available to spend on defence and on the protection of colonies overseas, at a time when the British empire in particular had grown to its greatest ever territorial extent. In the inter-war period, neither Britain nor France possessed the military or naval capacity to defend its empire across the globe, particularly if they faced a combination of enemies across different continents. By the 1930s, it was not just Bolshevik Russia which posed a serious challenge; Italian ambitions in the Mediterranean, Japanese aggression on the Chinese mainland and United States naval diplomacy were also causing great concern to British and French leaders. Thus historians now argue that the responses of the British and French governments to Hitler after 1933 have to be seen in the light of the complex and serious global challenges they were facing.

Historians such as Michael Howard in *The Continental Commitment* and David Dilks in his contribution to Adrian Preston's *General Staffs and Diplomacy before the Second World War* have stressed Britain's military weakness in the 1930s, and the fact that the three British military services were planning for three different wars. The British army was equipped to fight a frontier war in India, and had far more troops in Palestine between 1936 and 1939 than it had available to send to Europe; the air force was preparing for a bombing offensive against Germany; the navy was planning a war in the Far East against Japan. Baldwin and Chamberlain were repeatedly warned by their chiefs of staff that Britain did not have the military resources to contemplate war against Germany and Japan simultaneously if Italy was also hostile in the vital Mediterranean area. Chamberlain was active in the mid-1930s in supporting schemes of rearmament and in then pushing for the development of measures for air defence. At the same time he recognized the great dangers facing the British empire and the urgent need to try to come to terms with Mussolini or with Hitler in respect of their territorial claims.

French defence planning, as Robert Young has shown in *In Command of France* and in his chapter in *General Staffs and Diplomacy before the Second World War*, was geared to defence of the Maginot line and to the mobilization of resources to enable France to survive a long war of attrition. France's military forces were not organized for quick, offensive actions, and its political leaders therefore found it difficult to respond to Hitler's remilitarization of the Rhineland in 1936 without an extensive and time-consuming period of mobilization which was ruled out as being too provocative. French calculations that British aid would be vital in any future war led to acquiescence in Britain's reluctance to challenge Hitler in eastern Europe before 1939. At the fateful Munich conference in 1938, French leaders took the view that British support was more crucial than obligations to Czechoslovakia or to Poland. But, once these allies were lost, British support for France and involvement in eastern Europe became vital if resistance to Hitler was to be organized. And because of the multiple challenges facing the British empire in the 1930s, as well as lingering guilt over the perceived iniquities of the Treaty of Versailles, this support and promise of involvement were slow in coming.

Since the collapse of the Habsburg and Romanov empires at the end of the First World War, British leaders had perceived central

Europe to be an area of weakness, fragmented by the emergence of new states such as Czechoslovakia, Austria and Hungary. Already in the 1920s, Britain had shied away from any active involvement in the region or commitments to the new central and eastern European countries. Not only were they seen as unstable and economically weak; they also contained a volatile ethnic mix of peoples, including strong German communities who saw their future as lying inside an expanded Germany. There was from 1919 a strong feeling in Britain that the Treaty of Versailles had been unfair to Germany, not least because Wilson's celebrated nationality principles had been denied to the new Weimar republic. Thus successive British governments from 1919 onwards, preoccupied with safeguarding the empire and promoting economic recovery, sought to appease Germany and in due course to bring about peaceful revision of the Versailles settlement, particularly with regard to Germany's eastern frontiers, the stringent disarmament clauses and the occupation of the Rhineland.

The coming to power of Hitler was seen by many people in Britain to be a direct consequence of the failure of France before 1933 to agree to more than the most limited concessions to German revisionism. There was little surprise in Britain that Hitler denounced the Versailles restrictions on German armament levels and walked out of the League Disarmament Conference, that he aimed to remilitarize the Rhineland and that he sought *Anschluss* with Austria. British leaders certainly deplored the aggressive way in which he tore up the successive clauses of the Treaty of Versailles, but this made them only the more anxious to try to reach agreement with him over what they believed to be a limited set of Nazi objectives.

However, even though there is now a much greater understanding of and sympathy on the part of historians writing in the past twenty years for the appeasement policies pursued by Britain and France in the inter-war period, Neville Chamberlain remains a controversial figure. On the one hand there are historians, such as David Dilks, who believe that he did as much as he could to try to prevent the outbreak of another major war both by endeavouring to reach agreement with Hitler and at the same time by rearming and making it clear to Hitler that Britain would fight if Hitler continued his eastern expansion. In Dilks' view, 'We shall judge ministers of the 1930s more fairly if we conceive of them as men grappling with a deadly situation, contemplating the early outbreak of a war which they believed would be more horrible in its devastation and bloodletting than any previously recorded'. Chamberlain was very conscious of the fact that war had broken out to a large degree in 1914 because Germany had perceived itself to be encircled by the entente powers of France, Britain and Russia. He wanted to avoid making the same mistake again, and provoking Hitler to some 'mad dog act' by the adoption of strong deterrent policies on the part of Britain and France. At the same time Hitler was not an easy man to deal with; in a letter which Chamberlain wrote to his sister Ida in September 1938 he lamented, 'is it not positively horrible to think that the fate of hundreds of millions depends on one man and he is half mad?'

But, as his critics have not been slow to point out, Chamberlain was a stubborn and vain man, who genuinely believed that he could reason with Hitler and conclude an agreement with him which would safeguard European peace. He always thought he was right, and never mistaken; furthermore he hated opposition and criticism, and found it difficult to be agreeable to his critics. He was opposed to the consistent anti–German line taken by the permanent under-secretary in the British Foreign Office, Vansittart, and to the tendency of the Foreign Office, as he saw it, to view continuity of Prussian expansionism in every suggestion of Hitler. He removed Vansittart from the centre of foreign-policy decision-making, and surrounded himself instead by officials who shared his own outlook. He found Churchill's anti-Nazi tub-thumping grossly alarmist. Instead, he viewed Hitler as a 'man of moods' who, if reasoned with by such a consummate political operator as Chamberlain himself, 'would give you anything you ask for'. He told his sister that 'here was a man who could be relied on when he had given his word'. He genuinely believed that his three visits to Hitler in the autumn of 1938, culminating in the Munich conference, had secured 'peace in our time'. His optimism was not universally shared even at the time by his political colleagues; many historians continue to regard him as a short-sighted, dogmatic political leader, hopelessly naive and ill-informed about Hitler's personality and about the ideological beliefs and grandiose ambitions which were driving the German dictator. As Sidney Astor has written in his chapter in *Paths to War: new essays on the origins of the Second World War* edited by Boyce and Robertson, 'what emerges from the Chamberlain papers is misplaced trust, unwarranted optimism and erroneous judgements. Confidence in the ultimate success of appeasement . . . hindered Chamberlain's assessment of alternatives'.

Nonetheless the Munich agreements, which were condemned so strongly in earlier historical accounts, are now seen in a more favourable light as a result of evidence which has emerged in recent years showing that Hitler was fully prepared to resolve the Sudeten crisis by military action if he did not get his own way. Indeed, he believed that he had been outmanoeuvred by the scheming Chamberlain, and angrily resolved that he would not allow the British leader to foil his military intentions again over Danzig. Thus Chamberlain's diplomacy can now be seen to have had some success in the short term, and it gave Britain a further few months in which to rearm. By the time war finally came, in September 1939, following the Nazi invasion of Prague in March, the deadly threat which Hitler posed to Europe and to global stability could be clearly seen not just in Britain but throughout the British empire. Britain, its dominions and its colonies entered the war as a united force in 1939. As Michael Fry points out in his contribution to *The Munich Crisis, 1938*, edited by Lukes and Goldstein, that would certainly not have been the case had war come over the Sudetenland in 1938.

By early 1939 there was widespread opposition in Britain to the continuing appeasement of Hitler's expansionist ambitions. R.A.C. Parker tells us, in *Chamberlain and Appeasement: British policy and the coming of the Second World War*, that an opinion poll taken in February 1939 revealed that only 28 per cent of those polled thought that Chamberlain's policy would ultimately lead to enduring peace in Europe. He further points out that, by early 1939, there was 'a clearly stated alternative to the government's policy towards Germany. Where the government stressed conciliation towards Hitler . . . Chamberlain's opponents preferred "the language of the mailed fist". They wanted military alliances to encircle Germany, alliances dressed up in the language, and cloaked by the procedures, of the League of Nations'. And though, as we have seen, Chamberlain rejected this approach on the grounds that it would be more likely to provoke Hitler to military retaliation rather than to contain him, and because he had lost faith in the League's capacity to operate effectively after the failure of economic sanctions against Italy in the Abyssinian crisis, Hitler's occupation of Prague in March 1939 forced him to change tack. But he did so reluctantly, and only half-heartedly, offering a guarantee to Poland, Hitler's presumed next target, not as a declaration of serious intent to wage war if Hitler proceeded any further east but as a means of upping the stakes, and trying to induce the dictator to negotiate over Danzig and the Polish corridor rather than run the risk of a European war. As he later informed the House of Commons, this was 'not a policy of lining up opposing *blocs* of Powers in Europe . . . and accepting the view that war is inevitable'.

Those who remain strong critics of Chamberlain, such as R.A.C. Parker and Sidney Astor argue that he was too stubborn and too blinded by his prejudices to accept that by the end of 1938 coherent deterrence policies against Hitler offered the only means of preventing the outbreak of a European war. Parker's verdict on Chamberlain is a harsh one: he believes that it would have been possible for Chamberlain after March 1939 to secure sufficient support in parliament and in the country at large for a close alliance with France and for a policy of containing and encircling Germany within the framework of the League. Instead, 'his search for agreement with Hitler strengthened both Hitler's ambitions and his internal authority'. Under Chamberlain, according to Parker, the government 'rejected effective deterrence' and thus Chamberlain's obstinacy and skill in debate 'probably stifled' any serious chance of 'preventing the Second World War'.

This charge, which to some degree echoes the much earlier post-war interpretation of 'guilty men', rests very much on the assumption that effective deterrence could have been organized and led by the British government in the late 1930s. We have already seen that both British and French leaders were constrained in their responses to Hitler by the military weakness of their countries in the face of vigorous German rearmament, the scale of which, as we now know, both they and Hitler exaggerated. No League reprisals had been forthcoming to prevent German rearmament in the mid-1930s or to punish Germany in any way for flouting the provisions of the Treaty of Versailles over disarmament and the remilitarization of the Rhineland. Though the Soviet Union had become a member of the League of Nations in 1934 and was urging the formation of popular fronts across Europe to fight fascism, this proved to be a divisive rather than unifying theme, particularly in France and in Spain. The Spanish civil war, which broke out in 1936, drew in Italy and Germany to support Franco, and Soviet Russia and a motley collection of international brigades to support the republicans, with France and Britain reluctant to intervene. From a Russian perspective, the actions of its two fellow League powers up to the end of 1938, particularly during the Munich conference, did not suggest that they placed any great value on working in collaboration with Russia or had any intention of employing policies of deterrence against Hitler.

Thus the question we need to consider is whether by 1939 it would still have been possible for Britain and France to come to an understanding with Russia to enable the three powers to conclude a guarantee or military pact to contain Hitler. Suspicions were high on both sides, after nearly two decades of ideological warfare between communist Russia and the capitalist western powers. Substantial bodies of public opinion, in both Britain and France, saw communism as a greater danger than Nazism, and believed that any outbreak of major war would inevitably end in the triumph and expansion of Soviet Russia. Intelligence sources in both countries were aware of the relatively recent purges which had taken place in the Soviet Union, and the debilitating impact they had had on Soviet armed forces. Thus both governments were advised that, while Soviet troops could undoubtedly be counted on to defend Soviet territory, they had been seriously weakened as an attacking force. For his part, Stalin was intensely suspicious of the motives of Chamberlain and Daladier, believing that their intention was to fend off German military aggression to the west by encouraging the Nazis to expand eastwards. The Munich conference only confirmed him in this belief.

Looking back with the benefit of hindsight, it is very clear to see that Chamberlain's half-hearted efforts to woo Russia after March 1939 were doomed to failure. Chamberlain himself placed little value on Russian military power, and feared that attempts to co-operate with the Soviet Union would seriously complicate relations with Poland and Romania, to which Britain had just given military guarantees of assistance, and would gravely antagonize Germany. None the less, the guarantee to Poland forced the issue of Anglo-Russian relations to the fore, because, in the absence of Russian intervention, how could Britain help Poland militarily if the latter was attacked by Germany? As Lloyd George pointed out in the House of Commons in April 1939, 'Without the help of Russia, we are walking into a trap'. Chamberlain's attempt to frighten Hitler through the guarantee to Poland had the effect instead of increasing Russia's options. As Adam Ulam, in his study of Russian foreign policy between 1917 and 1973, *Expansion and Co-Existence*, claims, this guarantee made possible the train of events which led to the Russo-German pact of August 1939, since it gave the Russian government a freedom of manoeuvre that it would not otherwise have enjoyed. Stalin was able to play off Britain and France against Germany and to demand ever more binding agreements and terms, including the entry of Russian troops into Poland and Romania, which Britain felt unable to accept in the light of the strenuous refusal of both countries to agree to such 'assistance'. Though Chamberlain was willing to pursue negotiations with Russia into the summer of 1939, urged on by the British chiefs of staff who now strongly believed that only a full Franco-British-Soviet alliance would block a rival Nazi–Soviet understanding, he himself did not expect the talks to be successful. He wrote to his sister Hilda at the end of June 1939, 'My colleagues are so desperately anxious' for an agreement with the Soviet Union and 'so nervous of the consequences of failure to achieve it that I have to go warily but I am so sceptical of the value of Russian help that I should not feel our position was greatly worsened if we had to do without them'. At the same time, as Parker points out in *Chamberlain and Appeasement*, in *Pravda*, the official communist newspaper in Russia, Zhdanov was voicing his opinion that Britain and France 'do not want a real agreement or one acceptable to the USSR: the only thing they really want is to talk about an agreement, and by making play with the obstinacy of the Soviet Union, to prepare their own public opinion for an eventual deal with the aggressors'. Perhaps not surprisingly, by August Stalin decided that Soviet Russia's strategic interests were best served, at least in the short term, by a pact with Nazi Germany.

Could more vigorous British diplomacy, coordinated perhaps by someone such as Churchill, have prevented this outcome? There were enormous difficulties to be overcome, not least in the shape of strong Russian interests in eastern Poland, in Romania and in the Baltic states which Britain would never have found easy to accommodate. Furthermore, the Russians wanted guarantees about levels of armament to be deployed, which both France and Britain would have struggled to meet. And hanging over all these issues was the question of trust: could Stalin be trusted to keep to his side of the bargain, or would he at some point have been tempted by rival offers from Hitler? A policy of deterrence could work only if all three powers could identify clear interests in common, which would maintain strong bonds of unity. The challenge for Hitler would have been to try to break up any alignments which threatened to encircle Germany, and it is by no means certain that, had a pact been concluded between Britain, France and Soviet Russia, it would have remained in existence for long. We can certainly agree with Parker that there was no realistic chance of concluding such a pact, under Chamberlain's leadership. But it is less clear that a pact with Russia was feasible, or that it would have prevented war from breaking out. The evidence which is now available to us reveals very clearly the scale of Hitler's territorial ambitions and his ruthless determination to bring Germany to a state of readiness which would enable them to be achieved through military conflict. It is difficult, in the face of such evidence, to believe that he could have been contained by other European powers for very long, especially when he could call on the support of Italy and Japan to menace western interests in the Mediterranean and in the Far East. We also now have a much clearer, though by no means complete, picture of the emergence of Russian strategy in the mid- and late 1930s, which suggests that Stalin's overriding concern during this period was to safeguard Soviet interests. From his perspective, it was not entirely obvious by the end of 1938 that Britain and France would safeguard those interests more effectively than a deal with Hitler would.

There has been considerable debate about the factors shaping Soviet foreign policy in the 1930s. Was Russia sincere in trying to promote collective security policies through the League and through the formation of popular front coalitions to combat fascism? Or was this merely a façade, behind which secretive Soviet overtures were ever more insistently being directed at Nazi agents? Was Stalin's preference all along really for alliance with Hitler, as some historians such as Gerhard Weinberg and Robert C. Tucker have alleged? We know that there was sharp disagreement over Stalin's motives in Britain by the late 1930s. While some people were convinced of the sincerity of Russia's pursuit of collective security, others, notably Chamberlain as we have seen, regarded Russia's League diplomacy from the mid-1930s as 'a duplicitous attempt to divide Britain and France from Germany, provoke war and revolution, and pave the way for Soviet expansion'. Many historians now reject this interpretation, and argue that Stalin's foreign policy in the late 1930s, unlike Hitler's, was motivated not so much by his ideological beliefs but by his perception that, because the Soviet Union existed in an extremely hostile environment, it was vital to preserve its national security. As he told the 1934 Party Congress, 'We never had any orientation towards Germany, nor have we any orientation towards Poland and France. Our orientation in the past and . . . at the present time is towards the USSR and towards the USSR alone'. As Teddy Ulricks has argued, in his contribution to *Soviet Foreign Policy 1917–1991*, edited by Gabriel Gorodetsky, 'There was only one foreign policy line, both before and after 1933 and, for that matter, after August 1939. That line included the assumption of hostility from all of the imperialist powers and, therefore, the need to keep them divided . . . Throughout the decade, suspicion of all imperialist powers and a desperate search for security remained constant.' Geoffrey Roberts, in *The Soviet Union and the Origins of the Second World War*, endorses this view of the Soviet Union keeping its options open, negotiating for a military alliance with Britain and France but at the same time leaving open the door to Nazi advances. He believes that Stalin's doubts over Britain and France's commitment to a military guarantee grew as military negotiations progressed, and 'so the door to an agreement with Germany was opened wider. But not until the moment of the final breakdown of the military negotiations with Britain and France were the Germans invited across the threshold.' Patrick Finney's summary of Soviet motivations, in *The Origins of the Second World War*, is that

> The interpretation which best fits the evidence is that which sees Stalin mainly preoccupied with the search for security in a hostile capitalist world. Once Nazi Germany had obviously become the Soviet Union's chief potential enemy, Stalin launched the collective security campaign, yet prudence dictated that the door should be left open for the restoration of amicable relations with Berlin if German policy changed. By the same token, suspicion of the western powers never evaporated, and Stalin was determined not to be manoeuvred into a war with Germany from which Britain and France would stand aloof, and it was fear of this which finally provoked the Molotov-Ribbentrop Pact.

In the light of this consensus, it seems difficult to believe that Britain and France could ever have met Stalin's exacting price for a military alliance or completely dispelled his suspicions of western motives. It was much easier for Nazi Germany and the Soviet Union to come to an agreement which effectively assigned 'spheres of influence' in eastern Europe between the two of them, with each power harbouring an intention to build up power in its allotted sphere and to turn on the other when the moment was right.

If it was highly unlikely that Britain and France could work with the Soviet Union to contain Hitler, how realistic were Chamberlain's hopes, and those of Pierre Laval in France, of forming a common front with Mussolini against Nazi expansion? We know that, in 1934 and 1935, French leaders tried hard to court Mussolini and enlist him in the struggle against Hitler, but that their willingness to accommodate his African colonial ambitions, particularly through the infamous Hoare–Laval pact, fell foul of their undertakings as a League power. Equally, Chamberlain's attempts to make concessions to Italy in 1938 and to detach Italy from the Nazi camp, failed completely. To what extent was Mussolini open to diplomatic advances from Britain and France in the mid- to late 1930s? Or was he inevitably driven towards Hitler because of his fascist beliefs and admiration for the Nazi leader?

Historians of Fascist Italy continue to have conflicting views about the factors shaping Mussolini's foreign policy. Mussolini's Italian biographer, De Felice, has argued that, from the mid-1920s to 1935 and even beyond, Mussolini's overriding objective was to secure France's agreement to the establishment of Italy as a great power, with an expanded colonial empire in North Africa. In order to achieve this, Mussolini's advisers urged him to follow the 'policy of the decisive weight' in the European balance, or the 'policy of the pendulum' as it was called. This concept, also pursued by Liberal Italian governments before 1914, entailed, according to Dino Grandi, Mussolini's minister of foreign affairs, 'making one side or the other pay very dearly for our help at the right time'. The problem was that France, in the 1930s, was rarely prepared to pay a high price for Italian cooperation. As Pierre Guillen has observed, in his contribution to *French Foreign and Defence Policy, 1918–1940*, edited by Robert Boyce, the period saw

> a succession of phases of tension and . . . of rapprochement. The phases of rapprochement corresponded to the times when the French and Italians judged their interests to outweigh their differences and to warrant mutual concessions; the phases of tension were marked by French irritation in face of Italian claims, and by Italian disappointment at French refusal to take their claims into account. Generally speaking, these alternations occurred because,

although French leaders favoured an entente with Italy, they were not prepared to pay the price that Italy demanded.

So did Mussolini begin to edge closer to Hitler only after the Abyssinian crisis, when Britain had forced France to operate against Italian aggression within the machinery of the League of Nations and to agree to economic sanctions against Italy? There are historians who reject this interpretation, and who argue that Mussolini, far from keeping his options open and balancing Italian support between Britain and France on the one hand and Nazi Germany on the other, until at least the mid-1930s, had decided already in the 1920s on a more aggressive approach. MacGregor Knox argues, in his contribution to *The Origins of the Second World War*, edited by Patrick Finney, that in matters of foreign policy Mussolini was no pragmatic realist but an ideologue, driven by grandiose visions of Italian Mediterranean expansion. Knox informs us that Grandi repeatedly referred to the fact that 'Mussolini has an *unreal* conception of diplomacy. He calls this conception revolutionary, but the truth is that it is *unreal*'. In a striking extract from his diary, written in 1932, Grandi muses:

> I have asked myself why the Boss is so taken with Hitler. [Mussolini] has searched breathlessly for the last ten years or so, wherever they might be found, for 'allies' for a revolutionary foreign policy destined to create a 'new order' in Europe, a new order of which He considers himself the supreme Pontiff not only in the spiritual but also in the material sense . . . An international action founded exclusively on the Party, on the Regime, on a revolutionary ideology, not on the realism of the school of Cavour. *Mussolini does not love Cavour;* he never did.

In this interpretation, Mussolini aimed from the mid-1920s, according to Germany's ambassador in Rome in December 1924, Neurath, 'to make the Mediterranean a *mare italiano*. In that effort France stood in the way, and he had begun to prepare for battle with that adversary'. Mussolini believed that

> the situation in Europe created by the Versailles Treaty was untenable. In the new war between France and Germany that would therefore break out, Italy, led by Mussolini, would place

itself at Germany's side in order to crush France jointly. If that endeavour succeeded, Mussolini would claim as his booty the entire French North African coast and create a great *imperium latinum* in the Mediterranean.

So in this interpretation, Mussolini's eyes were firmly set on Italian territorial and colonial expansion from the mid-1920s, with a revisionist Germany his obvious partner. He wavered only momentarily from this course, in 1933 and 1934, as a result of aggressive Nazi intentions towards Austria, which could conceivably in the short term offer a serious threat to Italian security. But preparations for 'the total conquest' of Abyssinia none the less went full steam ahead, and Mussolini announced privately in 1935 that 'afterwards we shall conquer Egypt and the Sudan!' The fact that Italy lacked the economic and military strength to pursue Mussolini's grandiose vision effectively, and that it increasingly looked to Nazi Germany for assistance simply took the Italian dictator, it is argued, more quickly and more irrevocably to Hitler's side where he had long aimed to be. The Italian–German axis was strengthened by the involvement of the two powers in the Spanish civil war alongside General Franco, and, by the time Neville Chamberlain became prime minister in Britain, it was no longer possible, even if it might have been in earlier years, to negotiate concessions with Mussolini and wean him away from the Nazi camp. On this point, at least, there is agreement amongst historians of inter-war Italian foreign policy.

The wealth of evidence which is now available to us makes it abundantly clear that Hitler in Germany and Mussolini in Italy were determined to overturn the fragile territorial settlement which had been negotiated with such difficulty after the First World War, and that Bolshevik Russia was also committed to a revolutionary foreign policy from 1917 onwards. It is hardly surprising, therefore, that British and French leaders struggled to maintain international peace in the inter-war period, and lurched from crisis to crisis, anxious to avoid war but unsure of how this could be accomplished. Without doubt, many people in Britain underestimated the ideological fervour and aggressive intent of Nazi and Italian expansionist policies while at the same time fearing the threat of the spread of communism; they also feared the aerial bombardment and associated horrors that another war would inevitably bring, and found it difficult to believe that those who had experienced the agony of the First World

98

War could seriously be contemplating the outbreak of a second. Yet even those who did recognize from an early stage the deadly threat posed by Hitler's ambitions found it difficult to suggest a coherent strategy of deterrence, in the face of continuing Anglo-French disagreements, the weakness of potential allies in eastern Europe, the cumbersome machinery of the League of Nations in the face of German, Italian and Japanese hostility, and the enigma of communist Russia under Stalin. No wonder British and French statesmen struggled after 1933 to find answers to the mounting challenges posed by a group of powers intent on overthrowing the prevailing international order.

This brings into play the inter-war role of the United States. The failure of successive presidents, after Wilson, to engage in European diplomacy or to work with European powers to promote economic recovery undoubtedly increased considerably the problems facing those countries which were struggling to maintain European peace. The Wall Street crash, fuelled by domestic factors in the United States, set off an economic depression which had catastrophic consequences for Europe, not least in the emergence of Nazism as a serious political force in Germany. To what extent was the United States administration concerned about the threat posed to the European and international order by Hitler after 1933, and what actions did it take to try to prevent the outbreak of hostilities? Again there is considerable disagreement amongst historians about the different factors shaping American policies towards Europe in the 1930s, and about whether the aim of Roosevelt's administration was to conciliate Hitler or to contain him.

Some historians, such as Arnold Offner, in his contribution to *The Fascist Challenge and the Policy of Appeasement*, edited by Mommsen and Kettenacker, have argued that the United States sought to appease Hitler, and did not change this stance until 1940, by which time it had become abundantly clear to Roosevelt and his advisers that Hitler was beyond appeasement and was instead well on the way to constituting a serious threat to world order. The roots of this appeasement policy, it is argued, lay in antipathy to the Versailles peace settlement, a continuing mistrust of British and French intentions and some sympathy for German revisionist ambitions, many of which were seen as legitimate. Thus, according to this interpretation, American statesmen and emissaries to Europe in the mid- to late 1930s hoped to bring about a peaceful programme of modest political and economic change which would satisfy Nazi ambitions and be agreeable to the British and French governments. Despite Hitler's lack of interest and Chamberlain's reluctance to co-operate, Roosevelt persevered until after the German invasion of Poland in September 1939 in his unrealistic quest for peaceful change in Europe, not least because, in Offner's view, 'the United States was itself a revisionist power in Europe, pursuing an independently formulated policy of appeasement which was incompatible with those of Britain and France'.

Other historians disagree with this view of American policy and argue that Roosevelt did take steps in the later 1930s to try to contain German power through economic pressure. It is also argued, for example by Richard Harrison in his contribution to *Appeasement in Europe*, edited by Schmitz and Challener, that the President was fully alive to the dangers posed by German expansionism and tried to concert resistance towards Hitler but was frustrated by Chamberlain's determination to conclude a bilateral Anglo-German agreement. In addition, of course, Roosevelt had to work with a House of Representatives and appeal to an American public, large sections of both of which saw no advantage to the United States in becoming drawn into European affairs.

While British political leaders and Foreign Office officials in the inter-war period frequently referred to a 'special relationship' with America, and were conscious of the need to try to work co-operatively with the rising transatlantic world power, recent works on Anglo-American relations have stressed, in Finney's words, 'conflict rather than community of interest'. In this interpretation, significant differences divided the United States and Britain, not least conflicting views over the future of the British empire, and the American desire to pursue the 'Open Door' system as the basis of world trade in opposition to the British system of imperial preference endorsed by the Ottowa agreements. As Finney observes, 'Given these divergent interests, it was, perhaps, no surprise that the two powers failed to co-ordinate a policy towards Germany, whether of conciliation or resistance, until the pressing exigencies of war in 1940 temporarily suppressed their differences and facilitated a common front'.

The failure, for whatever reasons, of the two powers to work together was as significant in the Far East as it was in Europe. In east Asia, as in Europe, there was a power set on overturning the existing territorial order, and it was, in the last resort, Japanese aggression, rather than that of Nazi Germany, which finally brought the United States into the war in 1941. The extent of Japan's ambitions had become clear from the early 1930s, when, as Barnhart points out in *Japan and the World since 1868*,

Japan struck out on its own by leaving the League of Nations . . . in defiance of the old order of international relations. At the same time, its leaders, mainly its army, attempted to overthrow the old order within Japan, too. Japan's new order, therefore, would have two parts. Abroad, Japan would pursue an independent course, casting aside all hope of co-operating with the West. Manchuria . . . would be an integral part of the Japanese Empire. The rest of China . . . would fall under Japan's influence . . . The Soviet Union . . . would be neutralized by Japan's association with Germany, newly resurgent under Adolf Hitler and his National Socialist Party. Japan would use its acquisitions to build up a power base so great that no Western power would be able to challenge it in the future. Japan, in short, would at last be secure through the construction of its own vast empire. This ambitious international programme also required a new order within Japan.

Historians such as Richard Storry in *The Double Patriots* and W.G. Beasley in *Japanese Imperialism, 1894–1945* have graphically documented the ideological fervour which drove zealous Japanese patriots to reshape domestic politics within Japan in the period up to 1936, and which fed into ever-more ambitious schemes of Japanese imperial expansion.

Given British and French preoccupations with Europe, the Middle East and India, it was understandably difficult for the two powers to contain growing Japanese power in east Asia, though its longer-term menace to their Asian colonies and economic interests was clear to see. While Malcolm Kennedy has argued, in *The Estrangement of Britain and Japan, 1917–35*, that it was Britain's repudiation of the Anglo-Japanese alliance in 1922 'which severed Japan's old close ties with Britain and left her with a feeling of isolation and resentment', it is difficult to imagine that the continuation of this alliance would have prevented Japan from seeking to build up a strong sphere of influence and control in Manchuria and north China. Nor could it have offset the damaging impact to Japan of the depression, nor the radicalization of Japanese political and economic life which resulted. Thus the more important question is why it was not possible for the two western powers with the most extensive economic and colonial interests in the Far East, namely Britain and the United States, to work together to contain Japanese expansion. As in the European sphere, there was considerable misunderstanding and suspicion on both sides. During the Manchurian crisis in the early 1930s, the fact that Britain was trying to coordinate responses to the Japanese occupation of Manchuria through the League of Nations, whilst the United States insisted on operating through the Washington agreements of 1922, did not help to build up amicable relations. Whilst British officials weighed up the possible impact of economic or even military sanctions against Japan, the American administration would consider only 'the sanction of public opinion' and the weapon of 'non-recognition'. Each saw the other as selfish, as wedded to the pursuit of self-interest and as an unreliable partner. Again, it was not until the late 1930s, with Japan firmly entrenched on the Chinese mainland and aiming to expand southwards, that a growing sense of alarm and determination to take some action to challenge growing Japanese power brought Britain and America to work together more closely. The effect, however, was not to overawe Japan but to propel it into preemptive action, culminating in the *coup de grâce* against the American fleet at Pearl Harbor, and the entry of America into the war.

Thus even had the two powers found a basis for concerted action before 1940, it is by no means certain that earlier attempts at containment would have prevented the outbreak of hostilities in the Pacific. As with Hitler in Europe, firmer action at an earlier stage, rather than preventing war, might instead have precipitated it. What is now clear to us, seventy years later, is the strength of conviction and of ideological fervour which motivated both the Japanese ultra-nationalists and the Nazi leadership. The careful scholarship of historians of Japan in revealing the roots of inter-war ultra-nationalism has been matched in recent years by Ian Kershaw's magisterial and comprehensive two-volume biography of Hitler, which leaves us in no doubt that Hitler was intent on revolutionary change in Germany and on the reshaping of the international order to achieve German ascendancy. Only the most resolute action by a combination of powers acting in concert could have hoped to contain the combined ambitions of Japanese and Nazi fanatics and, in the wake of the Great War and its debilitating impact, such a strategy of deterrence was extremely unlikely to be adopted.

In the last resort, then, it could be argued that the origins of the Second World War, in Finney's words, lie in 'the destructive challenge posed by the revisionist powers to the international order established after the first world war'. As we know, large numbers of Germans never accepted the verdict of the First World War, and looked forward not so much to the overthrow of the Treaty of Versailles terms but to a renaissance of the German Reich and thence, they hoped, to a further round of fighting which Germany this time would win. Similarly, in Italy, a failure to secure what was felt to be its rightful share of territorial spoils from the war led to a nationalist backlash, the seizure of Fiume and the rise to power of Mussolini and the Fascist Party. Japan had entered the First World War to gain economic concessions and territorial rights on the Chinese mainland and in the north Pacific. After 1919 its governments sought to consolidate and to extend Japanese power by any means available. And, of course, potentially the most revisionist regime of all, Bolshevik Russia, arguably owed its existence to the strain of the First World War on the Romanov empire. Blood-curdling communist calls to subvert the existing capitalist order, which reverberated around Europe after 1917, could not fail to cause serious concern to political and economic leaders across the continent.

Those historians who refer to the 'thirty year' war, or, as Philip Bobbitt suggests in *The Shield of Achilles* to the Long War (which finally ended only in 1990), clearly have a strong case. Already in 1919, Foch could lament that 'This is not peace. It is an armistice for twenty years'. Taylor took up this theme in his *Origins of the Second World War* when he argued that another war had been implicit 'since the moment when the first war ended'. Ian Kershaw has argued persuasively that Hitler's combination of bullying and blackmail could not have worked 'but for the fragility of the post-war European settlement'. The Treaty of Versailles had left ethnic unrest in central and eastern Europe and an uneasy guilt complex in Britain. And the British and French publics wanted no second war. Yet nothing in history is inevitable. It is possible to see many points in the 1920s and 1930s when events might have turned out differently, and when an alternative choice of options might have led to a quite different result, with a range of knock-on effects. What is very clear to us now, in the face of a vast collection of primary evidence and the accumulating pile of secondary sources, is the complexity of issues and factors which shaped the inter-war world and which leaders and their advisers had to take into account. If some issues have become more clear-cut in the past seventy years, the diverse range of economic, strategic, geopolitical and social factors which historians now claim deserve to be taken into account has escalated alarmingly. Thus to reach definitive conclusions on the origins of the Second World War remains a daunting task, not just for the A level or university student but even for the most dedicated inter-war scholar. It is hoped that this chapter will have helped rather than have hindered this process.

4

Guide to further reading

General surveys

There are so many general outline surveys and collections of essays on the origins of the Second World War that it is difficult to know where to begin. A good starting point is Professor Richard Overy's *The Origins of the Second World War* (London, 1987), which can be supplemented with his *The Inter-War Crisis* (London, 1994). A thorough discussion of the different factors which need to be taken into account in any analysis of the outbreak of the war is P.M.H. Bell's *The Origins of the Second World War in Europe* (London, 1986). Slightly dated but still useful is Esmonde Robertson's edited collection of essays, *The Origins of the Second World War* (London, 1971), with contributions from A.J.P. Taylor, Alan Bullock, Hugh Trevor-Roper and Tim Mason amongst others. Clearly students will want to see why there was so much controversy over Taylor's interpretation by reading A.J.P. Taylor, *The Origins of the Second World War* (London, 1961; second edition, with new introduction, 1963). This should be read in conjunction with two stimulating collections of essays edited by Gordon Martel, *The Origins of the Second World War Reconsidered: The A.J.P. Taylor Debate After Twenty-Five Years* (London, 1986) and *The Origins of the Second World War Reconsidered: A.J.P. Taylor and the Historians* (London, 1999).

Recently published and reasonably concise outline accounts are A.J. Crozier, *The Causes of the Second World War* (London, 1997),

Victor Rothwell, *The Origins of the Second World War* (Manchester, 2001) and M. Lamb and N. Tarling *From Versailles to Pearl Harbor* (London, 2001). There are some useful essays in R. Boyce and E. Robertson *Paths to War : New Essays on the Origins of the Second World War* (London, 1989). Patrick Finney's reader, *The Origins of the Second World War* (London, 1997), brings together the work and contrasting interpretations of twenty historians on the origins of the war.

Books on Fascist and Nazi ideology

A good place to start here is with Walter Laqueur's *Fascism: A Reader's Guide* (London, 1979). More recent analyses are offered by Roger Griffin in *The Nature of Fascism* (London, 1991) and by Richard Thurlow in *Fascism* (Cambridge, 1999). Gerhard Weinberg's *The Foreign Policy of Hitler's Germany* (Chicago, Illinois, 1970) and *Germany, Hitler and World War II* (Cambridge, 1995) and Norman Rich's *Hitler's War Aims* (London, 1973) cast a lot of light on the expansionist ideology driving Hitler and Nazism. Ian Kershaw's *The Nazi Dictatorship: Problems and Perspectives of Interpretation* (London, 1985) is an indispensable guide to the debates amongst historians relating to the essence of Nazism and the factors shaping its foreign and economic policy.

Books and documentary collections on inter-war German history

One of the most comprehensive and accessible accounts of modern German history is Gordon A. Craig's *Germany 1866–1945* (London, 1978). Gordon Martel (ed.), *Modern Germany Reconsidered* (London, 1992) contains a very useful chapter by David Kaiser on 'Hitler and the Coming of the War'. John Hiden has written two helpful and succinct summaries, *Germany and Europe* (London, 1977) and *Republican and Fascist Germany* (London, 1996). Absolutely indispensable for students of the Third Reich is volume 3 of the documentary reader on Nazism edited by Jeremy Noakes and Geoffrey Pridham, *Foreign Policy, War and Racial Extermination* (Exeter, 1988). Students might also like to read the English translations of Hitler's *Mein Kampf* (with an introduction by D.C. Watt, London, 1974) and *Hitler's Secret Book* (with an introduction by Telford Taylor, New York, 1961).

Biographies

The definitive biography of Hitler is now Professor Ian Kershaw's magisterial two-volume study, *Hitler, 1889–1936: Hubris* (London, 1998) and *Hitler, 1936–1945: Nemesis* (London, 2000). Also still useful are Kershaw's *The Hitler 'Myth': Image and Reality in the Third Reich* (Oxford, 1987) and William Carr, *Hitler: A Study in Personality and Politics* (London, 1976). Whilst Alan Bullock's *Hitler: A Study in Tyranny* (London, 1952) is now very dated, his more recent, very lengthy study, *Hitler and Stalin: Parallel Lives* (London, 1991) has much of interest. The most recent English language biography of Mussolini is Denis Mack Smith's *Mussolini* (London, 1981).

Histories of Italy and of Russia

A good general history of Italy is Martin Clark's *Modern Italy, 1871–1982* (London, 1984). Also useful are Christopher Seton-Watson, *Italy from Liberalism to Fascism* (London, 1967) and C.J. Lowe and F. Marzari, *Italian Foreign Policy 1870–1940* (London, 1975). For more specific information on Mussolini's foreign policy there is D. Mack Smith, *Mussolini's Roman Empire* (London, 1976), J. Burgwyn, *Italian Foreign Policy in the Inter-War Period, 1918–40* (New York, 1997), E.R. Tannenbaum, *Fascism in Italy* (London, 1973) and M. Knox, *Mussolini Unleashed* (Cambridge, 1982).

On Russian foreign policy in the 1930s there are two very useful books by Geoffrey Roberts, *The Unholy Alliance: Stalin's Pact with Hitler* (London, 1989) and *The Soviet Union and the Origins of the Second World War* (London, 1995). Also of interest is J. Haslam, *The Soviet Union and the Struggle for Collective Security in Europe, 1933–9* (London, 1984). More general assessments of the Soviet Union under Stalin can be found in R. Tucker, *Stalin in Power: The Revolution from Above, 1928–41* (New York, 1990), Alec Nove, *Stalinism and After* (London, 1975) and Roy Medvedev, *Let History Judge* (London, 1971). A comprehensive survey of Soviet foreign policy can be found in Adam Ulam, *Expansion and Co-existence: A History of Soviet Foreign Policy, 1918–67* (London, 1968).

Appeasement policies: Britain and France, 1919–1939

The most recent survey of inter-war British foreign policy is Paul Doerr's *British Foreign Policy, 1919–39* (Manchester, 1998). The strategic and economic problems facing Britain in the inter-war period are well covered in Paul Kennedy, *The Realities Behind Diplomacy* (London, 1981), David Reynolds, *Britannia Overruled* (London, 1991) and Michael Howard, *The Continental Commitment* (London, 1972). The military historian Corelli Barnett offers a stimulating, if somewhat controversial, view of British decline in the inter-war period in *The Collapse of British Power* (Gloucester, 1984). The difficulties of defending the British empire after 1919 are outlined in A. Clayton, *The British Empire as a Superpower* (London, 1986) and in Paul Kennedy, *The Rise and Fall of British Naval Mastery* (London, 1976). The factors shaping British appeasement policies in the 1930s are assessed in William R. Rock, *British Appeasement in the 1930s* (London, 1977) and R.J.Q. Adams (ed.), *British Appeasement and the Origins of World War II* (Lexington, Kentucky, 1994). Chamberlain's role in the later 1930s is examined critically in R.A.C. Parker, *Chamberlain and Appeasement* (London, 1993) and in Frank McDonough, *Neville Chamberlain, Appeasement and the British Road to War* (Manchester, 1998). The difficulties inherent in the adoption of a policy of deterrence are examined in Wesley Wark, *The Ultimate Enemy: British Intelligence and Nazi Germany, 1933–39* (London, 1985).

There are two relatively recent studies of inter-war French foreign policy by Anthony Adamthwaite, *France and the Coming of the Second World War* (London, 1977) and *Grandeur and Misery: France's Bid for Power in Europe, 1914–1940* (London, 1995). French defence policy is clearly outlined in R.J. Young's two studies *In Command of France* (London, 1978) and *France and the Origins of the Second World War* (London, 1996). A very useful collection of essays is R. Boyce (ed.), *French Foreign and Defence Policy, 1918–40* (London, 1998). Anglo-French differences in the interwar period are well covered in P.M.H. Bell, *France and Britain 1900–1940 : Entente and Estrangement* (London, 1996) and in A. Sharp and G. Stone (ed.), *Anglo-French Relations in the 20th Century* (London, 2000).

Armaments and economic policies, 1933–1939

Some very useful studies of Nazi rearmament and economic policies have appeared in recent years. E.M. Robertson's classic study of *Hitler's Pre-War Policy and Military Plans* (London, 1963) has been followed by William Carr, *Arms, Autarky and Aggression* (London,

1972) and Wilhelm Diest, *The Wehrmacht and German Rearmament* (London, 1981). Two wider studies of Europe's readiness for war in the 1930s are Adrian Preston (ed.), *General Staffs and Diplomacy before the Second World War* (London, 1978) and D.C. Watt, *Too Serious a Business: European Armed Forces and the Approach to the Second World War* (London, 1975).

Nazi Germany's economic policies and their relationship to the outbreak of war have been comprehensively studied in David Kaiser, *Economic Diplomacy and the Origins of the Second World War* (Princeton, New Jersey, 1980) and in R.J. Overy, *War and Economy in the Third Reich* (Oxford, 1994). Professor Overy has also written a very useful study on *Nazi Economic Recovery, 1932–8* (London, 1982). Social issues are explored in two books by Tim Mason, *Social Policy in the Third Reich* (Oxford, 1993) and *Nazism, Fascism and the Working Class* (Cambridge, 1995).

Specific crises, 1935–41

A full-length study of the Rhineland remilitarization of 1936 can be found in J.T. Emmerson, *The Rhineland Crisis, 7 March, 1936* (London, 1977). The Abyssinian crisis is covered in G.W. Baer, *Test Case: Italy, Ethiopia and the League of Nations* (Stanford, California, 1977), in Frank Hardie, *The Abyssinian Crisis* (London, 1974) and in Chapter 5 of Ruth Henig (ed.), *The League of Nations* (Edinburgh, 1973). The definitive account of the Spanish civil war is Hugh Thomas, *The Spanish Civil War* (3rd edition, London, 1977), and its international impact is considered in M. Alpert, *A New International History of the Spanish Civil War* (London, 1994) and in Christian Leitz and David Dunthorn (ed.), *Spain in an International Context, 1936–1939* (Oxford, 1999). Two useful earlier works on the crises of 1938 are J. Gehl, *Austria, Germany and the Anschluss, 1931–38* (Oxford, 1963) and Keith Robbins, *Munich 1938* (London, 1968). More recent studies of the Sudeten crisis and of Munich diplomacy are Maya Latynski (ed.), *Reappraising Munich: Continental Perspectives* (Baltimore, Maryland, 1992) and Igor Lukes and Erik Goldstein (ed.), *The Munich Crisis, 1938* (London, 1999). Donald Watt, in *How War Came* (London, 1989), gives an extremely detailed picture of the diplomacy and politics of the period between the Munich conference and the outbreak of war in Europe. The period between September 1939 and the Japanese attack on Pearl Harbor is covered in William Carr, *Poland to Pearl Harbor: The Making of the Second World War* (London, 1985).

United States and Japanese foreign policy

Studies of American foreign policy towards Europe in the 1930s include David Schmitz and Richard Challener (ed.), *Appeasement in Europe: A Reappraisal of US Policies* (Westport, Connecticut, 1990) and Arnold Offner, *American Appeasement: United States Foreign Policy and Germany, 1933–38* (Cambridge, Massachusetts, 1969). Two differing views on Roosevelt's conduct of foreign policy can be found in Robert Dallek, *Franklin D. Roosevelt and American Foreign Policy, 1932–45* (New York, 1979) and in Frederick Marks III, *Wind Over Sand: The Diplomacy of Franklin Roosevelt* (Athens, Georgia, 1988). Relations between the United States and Britain in the later 1930s are well covered in David Reynolds, *The Creation of the Anglo-American Alliance, 1937–1941* (London, 1981), in Callum MacDonald, *The US, Britain and Appeasement 1936–9* (London, 1981), in Ritchie Ovendale, *'Appeasement' and the English-Speaking World 1937–1939* (Cardiff, 1975) and in William R. Rock, *Churchill and Roosevelt: British Foreign Policy and the United States, 1937–1940* (Columbus, Ohio, 1988). The Far East is the focus of Ian Cowman's *Dominion or Decline: Anglo-American Naval Relations in the Pacific, 1937–1941* (Oxford, 1996).

Japanese foreign and imperial policy is ably covered in Michael Barnhart, *Japan and the Wider World Since 1868* (London, 1997), in William Beasley, *Japanese Imperialism* (Oxford, 1987), in Akira Iriye, *Japan and the Wider World* (London, 1997) and in Ian Nish, *Japanese Foreign Policy, 1869–1942* (London, 1977). Richard Storry gives a vivid picture of 1930s Japanese ultra-nationalist ideology in *The Double Patriots* (Boston, Massachusetts, 1956). The Manchurian crisis and its aftermath is ably examined in Christopher Thorne, *The Limits of Foreign Policy* (London, 1972) and in Dorothy Borg, *The United States and the Far Eastern Crisis, 1933–38* (Cambridge, Massachusetts, 1964). Sino-Japanese relations in the later 1930s are covered in Youli Sun, *China and the Origins of the Pacific War, 1931–41* (London, 1993) and the best general survey is to be found in Akira Iriye, *The Origins of the Second World War in Asia and the Pacific* (London, 1987).

Index

threat to British Empire 1920s
86
USA. xiv, 3, 5–7, 10, 13–14, 25,
67, 72, 83–6, 110; attitude to
League of Nations 43; factors
shaping inter-war foreign policy
99–101, 110; lend-lease act,
1941 63; neutrality act, 1935 46;
'open door' economic policy
100; position in Far East,
1940–1 62–3; reaction to
Manchurian crisis, 1931–3 36,
102; Senate rejection of
Versailles settlement, 1919–20
10, 86; Wall Street crash, 1929
14, 99; Washington Naval
Treaty, 1922 34
Upper Silesia 8
Urals 85

Vansittart, Robert 89
Versailles peace settlement, 1919 1,
6, 8–10, 12, 15, 17, 24–6,
29–31, 33, 40–2, 65, 70, 76, 82,
87–8, 91, 97, 99, 103

Vichy xiv, 59
Vienna 9, 19–20, 49–50
Victor Emmanuel II of Italy 3

Walloons 27
Warsaw 58
Washington 62; naval conference,
1921–2 25–6, 32, 34;
agreements 102
Weiszacker, Ernst von 57
Wilson, Horace 53
Wilson, Woodrow 10, 86, 88, 99;
fourteen points of 9
World War I 1–2, 5–7, 10,
19–20, 27, 34, 42, 47, 59, 65,
67, 70–1, 75–6, 85–7, 98,
103
World War II 2, 68, 82, 91, 106,
109–10; origins of 1, 5–7, 65,
70, 72, 77, 102, 104–10

Yugoslavia 12, 29

Zhdanov, General 93
Zinoviev, Grigoriy 86